CONTE~~NTS~~

Acknowledgements

The Aware Manager is a sequel to *The New Manager* published by Element Books in 1988 and as such uses some similar material as its source. Again, as a book written for busy people who do not have resource to academic libraries, it would be unwise for us to include references that are difficult to locate, however, in fairness some of our sources for this book are to be found only in erudite journals and these do need to be acknowledged.

Chapter 2
Born to Win Muriel James and Dorothy Jungewald (Addison-Wesley 1971) – an initial and readable guide to the work of Eric Berne. A book in less popular style is *TA Today* by Ian Stewart and Vann Joines, Lifespace 1987.

Chapters 3 & 4
Many assertiveness training texts are written for women and these have certainly affected our thinking:
A woman in her own right Anne Dickson, Quartet and *When I say No I feel guilty* Manual J. Smith, Bantam. *Body Language* Allan Pease, Sheldon 1981, will provide an exciting addition to our thinking. *Assertion Training*, Anni Townsend, published by the FPA Education Unit, 1985 acts as a trainer's guide. We also quote from Kipling's *IF*.

Chapters 5 & 6
Ideas come from *The Rational Manager*, Kepner and Tregoe, McGraw Hill, 1965 and *Experiential Learning*, David Kolb, Prentice Hall, 1986. It also leans on the concepts of Barbara Carlsson and her Co-workers of Proctor and Gamble and published as *R & D organisations as Learning Systems*, Sloan Management Review, Spring 1976.

Chapter 7
Is based on the work of Victor Vroom and an article *A New Look at Managerial Decision Making*, Organisational Dynamics, Spring 1973, published by the American Management Association, New York.

THE AWARE MANAGER

Mike Woods is a lecturer with the Post Experience Programme unit of Bradford University Management Centre and is a Director of Management Development Workshops Ltd, developing courses and training working managers.

His particular interests include change management, the special problems of the newly appointed manager and assisting established managers towards more effective personal and professional development. The companies with whom he is currently working include BP, Croda Chemicals, Douglas Holdings, GKN, Hawker Siddeley, Shell and Unilever.

He is a training associate of Leeds University Psychology Department (CCDU), where he is currently involved with helping teachers to adjust to the current changes in British education. He is also an adviser on change to a major UK charity and has worked with the DHSS/DSS to similar purpose. He has appeared in and worked on several television programmes on Assertive Behaviour.

By the same author

THE NEW MANAGER

A guide to improving the skills of people
management for newly appointed managers

THE AWARE MANAGER

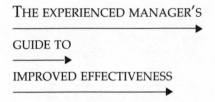

THE EXPERIENCED MANAGER'S

GUIDE TO

IMPROVED EFFECTIVENESS

Mike Woods

 ELEMENT BOOKS

First published 1989 by
Element Books Limited
Longmead, Shaftesbury, Dorset

Typeset by Photoprint, Torquay, Devon

Printed and bound in Great Britain by
Billings, Hylton Road, Worcester

Designed by Jenny Liddle
Cover design by Max Fairbrother
Cover illustration by Peter Till

British Library Cataloguing in Publication Data
Woods, Mike
The aware manager.
1. Management
I. Title
658

ISBN 1–85230–078–7

Chapter 8
Develops from the concepts of Mervin Weisbord and includes work by Tuckman. The direct quotation is from *Starting a High Technology Company – Strategies for success*. Deloitte Haskins and Sells High Technology Group, October 1985.

The distant origins of Chapter 9 have been published as *The ecology of organisations and the concept of the acceptance of change*, M.F. Woods and S. Hyde in R&D Management, Vol. 10, No. 1, Oct. 1979 and in *Creativity Week* of the same year by The Center for Creative Leadership, North Carolina.

AUTHOR'S NOTE

This book, as was *The New Manager*, is written by a working trainer, and as such will inevitably contain material from many sources. The principal influences are acknowledged gratefully and include Berne, Kepner and Tregoe, Vroom and Yetton, de Bono, O'Connel, Kolb and Tuckman. Many significant communicators have planted seeds that have perhaps germinated in a way that they may only just recognise, most notable of these being Bernard Haldane, Barbara Carlsson, George Davies and Marvin Weisbord. There is also material culled and developed in my work with other trainers, notably Mike Fordham, Beryl Heather, Marje Allen, Mike Carpenter and generically from association with the Career Counselling and Development Unit of Leeds University Psychology Department. As we have said previously, if you recognise more of your ideas than you think fit, please let us know so that we may acknowledge your contribution in later editions. In the meantime, I, Mike Woods on behalf of the Element Books team, apologise.

The characters that appear in this book – Adam, Betty, Campbell, Dennis . . . are completely fictitious in that they are composites designed to make a point, and again we apologise if you recognise more of yourself than you think fit.

The company case studies are based on publicly available sources or from my own work as a consultant. The view and interpretations of events are entirely mine and hopefully will be taken as those of an outsider who wishes the insiders well. In all cases remedial action, where necessary, has been taken by those concerned.

CHAPTER ONE

The Period of Adjustment

A manager new to the job of managing – coming perhaps from the shop-floor or from some expert or crafts role in an organisation – needs to adjust to the organisation. New things are required of him or her and new motivations are needed in the short and medium term.

Adam had left school without any significant qualifications and worked on the shop-floor of a major engineering company. The company policy was to offer employees formal training in the local technical college, and Adam, with this training, found a new potential which was rewarded by an offer of a job in the drawing office. He accepted the offer and found himself with a new white coat and a draughtsman's table on the second floor. As was pointed out by the company personnel manager at the time, the money would not be better since he would lose paid overtime but the prospects were, good and there would also be the immediate advantage of being on a monthly salary and not having to work to the clock.

Adam spent the first few weeks adjusting to his new position. On the social side he found that his usual lunchtime game of football was impossible because of the different break times. He also found that his new office was a 'no smoking' area. He regretted the loss of the football but he welcomed the excuse to stop smoking – he was saving to get married. There were several other little adjustments he had to make.

More seriously he missed certain aspects of his previous job. He had been a highly skilled fitter who was the recognised expert in interpreting 'vague' areas in technical drawings, and it was perhaps this skill, along with his technical college results, that had got him his transfer to what he perceived as the first stage of the management ladder. From being the respected expert among his peers he became the beginner. Gradually he found that the white collar work of the drawing office and the blue collar work of the fitting shop were fundamentally the same. He was still producing something tangible against instructions to set criteria and with gaining confidence, he could take a pride in his own growing skills. Soon, however, he achieved a new role in the office, it was remembered that he had been able to sort out the 'vague' items of drawing on the shop-floor and he became recognised in the office as a person who could prevent the 'vague' items going to the shop-floor in the first place. He became an informal arbitrator for his colleagues' work – 'will the fitters understand this or do I have to spell it out?' His informal supervisory role got him promotion to Assistant Manager grade and a trainee who needed to be coached in the ways of a draughtsman.

Adam in our case study, both as a fitter and as a draughtsman, used his skills to work with resources towards a defined goal – that was until he was promoted to management. The job of any manager is the direction of resources, including people, towards a goal, and real change comes when we cease to be a 'worker' and become a manager. From doing things ourselves we have to allocate resources, facilitate, motivate and get *others* to produce. My previous book, *The New Manager*, dealt with the issues of adjustment from 'worker' to manager. The present book will move ahead in the careers of the Adams and Eves of this world to the point in their lives when they would begin to call themselves experienced managers.

For the experienced manager the novelty of command has grown thin and there has come an awareness of 'could do better'. The awareness may have come from formal and informal appraisal by their peers and their bosses but most importantly it will have come from themselves. In this book we are talking to such experienced managers who are effective most of the time but recognise frustrations when things do not go right – when the bad performer remains the bad performer and the boss still expects the impossible and does not always get it. The purpose of this book is to help skilled managers do the job that little bit more effectively and gain wisdom to better satisfy their own exacting demands and allow them to grow in the job.

The issue we have found with hundreds of experienced managers is that it is always difficult to classify the factors preventing getting the extra 10 per cent of satisfaction that comes from a job done well rather than merely adequately. Often we hear the same words:

'I know exactly what I should have done . . .'

The speaker may be talking about standing up to the boss and not agreeing to an impossible delivery date or he or she may be regretting not having recorded an informal reprimand for lateness to a basically unsound subordinate – but it is not always so. We also meet many managers who can say with justification:

'There was nothing I could have done, even with hindsight.'

The examples we have had quoted to us include managers who have had to work with people who are blatantly exploiting their position or may simply not be up to their jobs. We have also been told of occasions when managers find themselves trapped in organisations destined to fail in spite of their best efforts. It is here the manager begins to think the game is no longer worth the candle.

The British television manufacturer Fidelity PLC survived the Pacific Basin invasion of electronic products until the beginning of 1988. The shop-floor and the management worked together to increase quality and decrease production costs in spite of the obvious wage-rate advantage of Korea, Taiwan . . . As it became more and more difficult to obtain part-finished goods and in particular TV tubes from UK suppliers, they had to seek these from abroad. Fidelity PLC managers, through quite vicious personnel policies, survived the fact that the essential components they had to import were taxed but that their competitors were able to import whole TV sets free of duty. However, the last straw came when the £ sterling continued to rise against the US dollar – the factory was forced to close. Management estimated the rise of sterling over six months took over £20 off the landed priced of an imported TV set retailing at less than £150.

The Fidelity brandname is now owned by Alan Sugar's Amstrad.

The managers of Fidelity PLC may have had difficulties as managers, although the evidence is that they were personally very effective – it was 'THEM', it was the outside world that defeated Fidelity and forced the managers to recommend the closure of the factory.

In this and following chapters we will be attempting to answer the multiple question:

'Is it us, is it *them*, and more seriously
– do we still want to play?'

We will look at the main issues that make all of us less than perfect in our professional dealing with others. We will consider how we may react inappropriately in crisis and how we are inclined to find certain situations that drive us into what we will term 'catastrophe spiral' – everything we do only seems to make it worse and finally the 'worst' happens. We will look at the vexed subject of 'meetings' and how individuals differ in what they perceive as their contributions. We will take these differences and develop issue on interviewing, recruitment, briefing, supervision and motivating. Next we will discuss the manager as a leader and how teams may be more effectively developed. From this point we take successive steps back to the management job and finally to the manager within the organisation. Our final view of the manager as a cog in the total world of the organisation will allow the Aware Manager to understand, predict and hopefully reduce the chances of having to live through situations such as the sadness that was Fidelity PLC.

Before we start on the main burden of the book it would seem sensible to look at the management jobs we are performing and ask ourselves whether we are in the right job in the first place. We will then move onto attempting to define the boundaries of our work.

--------------➤

EXERCISE

Think of two incidents which occurred to you acting in your role as a manager and which you can recall with a certain fondness.

When you think back, do *not* limit your choice to formal management incidents – you may well have been acting as a manager when you worked for a local Scout Troop or even by helping at the scene of a motorway accident – the test is that you can look back on the incidents with pleasure and say to yourself:

'I am proud of that, it may not be much to other people but I still remember it as a time when I derived real satisfaction from using my skills effectively. It was good.'

Ideally, we would like you to explain the incidents to a colleague, but failing that, write down the salient facts. Do not be ashamed about claiming your contribution to the incidents and make sure you detail how you felt and what you actually did. What 'skills' did you use? Think and record how you assessed your own personal satisfaction and consider why these were among your 'valued' experiences.

Now review what you have recorded and look at the overall criteria of judgement that made you choose this particular situation and in particular the skills you employed –

> If you can keep your head when all about you
> are losing theirs and blaming you . . .
> If you can meet with Triumph and Disaster
> And treat those impostors just the same . . .
> If you can talk to crowds and keep your virtue . . .
>
> *If* – Kipling

Kipling has listed his own set of valued skills, but they may not fit our own fondly remembered experiences.

⟶

The question we are leading to concerns your 'bread and butter' management job and we are going to ask you how many of the skills you valued from your fondly remembered experience you use regularly in your existing job.

Let's give examples of two managers, Betty and Campbell, both of whom work from the UK and were asked to recount incidents they remembered with a certain fondness and where they felt effective as managers.

Betty told us of one particular incident. She was bringing her family home from holiday by car and as she pulled up to a petrol station quite late on a Friday afternoon one of her children noticed that the car radiator was losing water. The petrol station attendant directed her to the nearest agent for her car – a Ford, and she arrived about an hour before they were closing the service facility for the weekend. The agents unfortunately did not have a spare radiator available but suspected that the main agents, some 10 miles up the road, would be able to supply and fit. Betty asked the service engineer to ring up the main agents, clear that the spare was available and would be ready for her and her exhausted family in about twenty minutes. She offered to pay for the telephone call but her offer was declined. The service engineer, in spite of having obviously completed a hard day, was very enthusiastic and insisted on providing a detailed map of how to get to the main agents. Betty also felt a certain respect from him for the way she had handled the issue.

The leaking radiator, car and its passengers arrived at the main agents exactly as planned and with the car just at the point of disaster. The radiator and a mechanic were waiting and the job was completed at a very reasonable cost exactly five minutes before the whole station closed for the weekend and exactly as Betty had planned. Betty felt very good about it.

Campbell's fondly remembered incident was quite different.

Campbell had been with his present company for five years and during that time as Operations Manager he had turned the unit round financially. By working 60 to 100 hours a week he had converted an apathetic workforce into what he described as a 'fighting unit' capable of taking on anyone in the industry – 'including the Pacific Basin'. However, he had been very tough and had begun by sorting out the 'laggards' and did not expect to be liked.

On his 38th birthday he arrived back from a business trip just before the lunch-break and the shop-floor was empty. He was met by his secretary, who said that he was wanted urgently in the canteen. The canteen was full of his staff and a massive 38-candle birthday cake. He cried to himself but managed not to show it.

Let's look at the incidents Betty and Campbell presented and see how they differ in the way each of them value using their real skills. From our previous knowledge, both Betty and Campbell are effective managers and show as much in their chosen 'valued incident'. However, the incidents show a very different pattern of attitudes and behaviour. Although, looking at the way Betty and Campbell work, they may employ a vast range of overlapping skills, in their choice of 'fondly remembered incidents' the sub-set, the range of skills employed is much more restricted.

If we review our work we will be able to remember certain times when we felt good about what we were doing.

On these occasions very often we are employing a sub-set of our personal skills.

Employing this sub-set of personal skills creates the jobs we find satisfying.

We are postulating that as experienced managers, we are all attempting to manoeuvre our jobs to give more personal satisfaction – towards being as pleasant as our 'fondly remembered incidents'. We attempt to choose the most suitable job in the first place but our currency for manoeuvre is our 'valued skills' – we try to use as many of these 'valued skills' as possible in our jobs and sometimes the end-product of our manoeuvre is not, in the widest sense, appropriate.

Let's see how the process could work and see how the differences in 'valued skills' can become critical. To do this we will get Betty and Campbell to apply for the same job – heading a management information service to a large company.

If we look at Betty's valued skills first we need to look both at what she includes in her account and what she leaves out. The explanation of her 'fondly remembered incident' and the subsequent discussion tell us that Betty enjoyed using her ability to respond to the unexpected – she was effective in a crisis and enjoyed it. She derived immediate satisfaction from the way in which she was able to organise/motivate very ordinary people to do quite unusual things for her and accept the silent admiration of the ordinary people who watched it happen. She did not expect to get praise from the family and in fact would probably accept the criticism that the incident need not have happened in the first place had she planned ahead. She was good at being clear-headed in a crisis, at planning under pressure, and co-ordination. She valued her enthusiasm and single-mindedness to pull through the crisis and in a single word, her skill of flexibility. Her 'skill' of frugality was also valued in that she would not remember the incident so fondly had she ended up 'buying herself out of the problem'.

Campbell shows a completely different set of personally valued skills. His 'fondly remembered incident' is about using his skills of hard work, stamina and integrity. He values his leadership skill and does not expect to be liked when he pushes – himself and his staff. He would describe himself as a 'manager of the old school' and has the dedication, loyalty and toughness designed for the long haul. The respect he got from his staff and the surprise reward from *his* people confirmed his own values – a pleasant experience for anyone.

Now think of the things that Betty and Campbell do not include in their incidents. Betty is talking about solving immediate problems and what could – perhaps unkindly – be called – *crisis management*. She is enjoying challenge and she is *not* talking about 'long hauls' and 'stability', although she may well possess skills in these directions should the situation call for them. She talks about the instant feedback of recognition by the service engineer in the first garage for her skill in controlling a difficult situation. Campbell talks almost from the opposite perspective. He is talking about rewards for hard work coming as a pleasant surprise. Campbell valued in himself stamina and endurance and although he may well possess flexibility, he does not value it as does Betty. Both are 'good' managers, but let us now think of the way they will manipulate their jobs to give themselves most rewards.

> We are saying that managers attempt to mould their daily work so that they can use the skills they personally value.

All of us attempt, albeit quietly, to use as many of the skills we value as possible and restructure our jobs accordingly. Conversely, the use of the skills we may possess but that give us limited satisfaction will receive low priority. We can do little about 'what turns us on' personally but we can recognise that those around us are different. Betty's valued incident was made up of her using a personal portfolio of skills which are certainly only a sub-set of her total portfolio of skills. Betty may well be able to maintain stability in a long-haul situation, but she is unlikely to find it a pleasurable experience and the skills she will use will not be highly rated by her. She is likely to find using such skills boring, and unless she is very careful the people around her who use such skills could be seen by her as being boring as well. Those working for and around her will certainly recognise her set of values and the net effect could well detract from her management performance. Campbell, on the other hand is certainly able to handle snap decisions in a crisis but he will probably regard such behaviour as 'a temporary expedient'

> We shape our jobs, given the opportunity, to best employ the skills whose use we find personally rewarding.
>
> By valuing certain skills in ourselves and denigrating other skills we may well possess, it is easy to denigrate other people.

and not honour either his own skill in making snap judge-ments or those around him who can. Betty could well find him as an unsympathetic manager, while Campbell would find Betty 'erratic'.

We choose or attempt to mould our jobs so that the jobs allow us to use our valued skills and get the corresponding personal satisfaction. On this basis in an ideal world Betty will find a 'challenging' job where her ability to prosper in change will be rewarded. Almost conversely, in an ideal world, Campbell will look for a job 'he can get his teeth into' and stamina will be rewarded. It is not difficult to imagine both Betty and Campbell finding themselves in jobs where their style of adaptation of the job could be disastrous for themselves and the organisation they serve. Betty would get bored and engineer crisis and Campbell might well hope that problems will go away and not interfere with the smooth running of his ship.

> We are aware of warmth and like flowers,
> we attempt to move towards the light. We work
> best at those things that we value most.

Think of the whole process in the form of a sequence:

Stage 1
We choose a job
which in the
circumstances
most fits our
needs and expectations.

Stage 2
We move into the job
and adapt our own
behaviour.

Stage 3
We begin to attempt
to modify the job
so that our valued
skills are used.

> Stage 4
> We reach a balance
> determined by the
> job and our valued
> skills.
>
> > Stage 5
> > We or others
> > decide whether
> > the compromise
> > is valid.

Let's see where we can move from here and look at Betty and Campbell in a job – not just isolated 'fondly remembered incidents', but the total world of work. We are not saying that the Aware Manager ceases to adapt to the job at any stage but we are saying that the process of balancing valued skills against the abstract concept of required skills soon becomes important. Imagine Betty and Campbell have put in for the job of running a management information team in a large company (see opposite).

It sounds like quite a job.
The first thing we will do is to translate the job as specified in the imaginary advertisement into elements:
We would see these elements as:

1 Psychological support for the group
2 Management and control of the various group activities
3 Communication within the group and to outsiders
4 The training and support
5 Specific problem-solving operations

If we knew a great deal more about the job than appears in the advertisement we could now draw up an ideal skill/attribute profile and see how Betty and Campbell shape up (see page 12). The questions we will ask are not simply, 'Can they do it?' but 'Will they use skills or attributes they value in doing it the way it needs to be done?' We will simply rate the skills High, Medium or Low.

There are several issues coming out of the analysis of the list. Firstly, I would doubt whether the most sophisticated psychometric procedure would claim to be able to produce such an

MANAGEMENT INFORMATION
CO-ORDINATOR

The job is to provide management information for the Research and Development function of a large multinational and reports directly to the Head of Laboratory.

There are various strands of the work, which include:

- The provision of up-to-date information on projects both within and externally to the group. A fully computerised system has been operating for some time but needs to be continuously refined to meet the specific changing and growing needs of all levels of the business.

- Basic support and training for R&D personnel, many of whom are specialists in very restricted areas.

- The preparation of formal and informal reports and documents reporting the work of the whole group in the area of change and change management.

- The day-to-day control of internal and external consultants working within the function.

The salary is negotiable and commensurate with experience.

The Company is an Equal Opportunity Employer.

Write to John Doe, Company Personnel, PO Box 234, London for an application form.

Assessment of Betty and Campbell against the Management Information Co-ordinator job.

	Betty Attribute/ Skill H-M-L	Valued H-M-L	Campbell Attribute/ Skill H-M-L	Valued H-M-L
Psychological support				
Focus on change	H	H	M	H
Charisma	H	H	H	L
Informal counselling	L	M	L	L
Ombudsman	M	L	H	L
Chairperson	H	H	H	L
Management and control				
Numerate	M	L	H	H
Understanding of budgets	M	M	M	M
Lieutenant	H	L	M	H
Liaison	H	H	H	M
Trustworthy	M	M	H	H
Low personal ambition	H	L	M	M
Methodical	L	L	H	H
Accurate	L	L	H	H
Just	M	H	H	H
Communication				
Multi-disciplined	H	H	M	L
Credible	M	L	H	H
Talking and writing	H	H	M	H
Secretary	M	M	M	M
Discreet	L	L	H	H
Serendipity	H	H	L	L
Training				
Contacts	H	H	M	M
Organisation	L	M	H	H
Political ear	M	L	M	M
Trainer	H	H	M	H
Problem-solving				
Logic	M	L	H	H
Creativity	H	H	M	M
2 ears/1 mouth	M	M	H	M
Trustworthy	M	M	H	H
Self-starter	H	H	H	M

analysis for anybody in an interview/appraisal situation without an amazing level of co-operation. We would, however, see any Aware Manager being able to produce one for themselves – and then perhaps not making it public.

Secondly, apart from one's peers, there are three 'people' concerned in any management situation – yourself, your sub-ordinates and your boss. If you do not have a particular skill but need to manage those who do, the way in which you value that particular skill is important. Thus Campbell does not possess the skills of a trainer but he does value the skill and hence could be perceived as a manager able to *motivate* trainers. Betty, however, neither possesses nor values the skills of numeracy, logic or accuracy and since the job will certainly involve her in the management of people who both need and value such skills, she and her staff could well have a problem. It will mean a real effort on her part not to underrate such members of staff who do value and have to use such skills and not allow them to feel less in her eyes than those sharing her own set of valued skills. Her own adaptation to the job and her adaptation of the job towards the skills whose use she finds personally rewarding could involve a very fine balance in these areas.

From the boss's point of view we have the immediate problem of selection – who will do the job best, and in the way that is closest to the way it *needs* to be done, regardless of the way they feel it *should* be done?

———————▶

EXERCISE

Who, if either, would you appoint for the job as advertised?

What criteria are you adopting for this decision?

In considering Betty and Campbell for a job we are also considering ourselves. Let's look at our own jobs.

Look at the elements of your own job, very much as we structured the fictitious job for Betty and Campbell.

Look at the skills necessary to perform your own job in the elements and classify them as High/Medium and Low.

Measure your own skills against this list both as 'possessing' and as 'valuing'.

Consider the discrepancies:

Do you have gaps that are not filled by subordinates?

Where you do have subordinates filling the gaps, and you do not value the skill in yourself, does this produce problems?

Looking back at the structuring of your job and the analysis, are you happy that the inevitable compromise between your own leanings and the appropriate way of structuring the job is reasonable?

──────────▶

Summarising, we have seen that there is a possible discrepancy between what we value doing and what we could do if pushed. The Actual Skills vs Valued Skills balance is vital to us as individuals and as managers. The point at issue is that we may be able to do things, but unless we get some sort of kick from doing them, we are inclined to find some more personally valued things to do.

An experienced manager will be well along the road of the process of adapting his or her behaviour to the job and is now struggling to find a balance between the job as presented and the job which gives most personal satisfaction. We have looked at some of the pressures coming from the manager and from the organisation that affect the balance.

In the next chapter we will establish how we as individuals perform in the role of manager, both 'on a good day with the wind on our side' and under pressure, and will relate this potential change in position to our relations with peers, bosses and subordinates.

CHAPTER TWO

'On a Good Day with the Wind on my Side'

'On a good day with the wind on his side I know where I am with my boss, but under pressure it's as if I'm talking to a different person.'

In the last chapter we discussed the way in which we initially adapt to our jobs and ultimately attempt to adapt our jobs to ourselves, reaching in many cases an unhappy balance of what we want to do and what we are required to do. Many, if not all, of the Aware Managers we know continue to learn in their jobs and the process of adaptation carries on throughout their careers. We also find, however, that the process whereby the job is shaped to the individual must be considered. The shaping of the job to the job-holder may not always be appropriate and can reduce the ability of individuals and organisations to respond to change. The best advice I personally have ever accepted was:

'WHEN YOU CEASE TO LEARN, THEN YOU LEAVE.'

In this chapter we will look at States of Mind from which your behaviour is born and how the balance of your states of mind may change with outside pressure.

Before we begin we would like you to complete the Personal Response Inventory and come up with an X and Y score for yourself.

PERSONAL RESPONSE INVENTORY

Imagine yourself in the following situations and consider your likely responses. You have 10 points for each situation and these should be allocated between the alternatives listed, giving the largest number of points to the response most fitting your own likely behaviour.

EXAMPLE

When I meet a group for the first time:

2 I wonder whether they are my sort	**0** I try to make them feel at ease	**4** I check out names and roles
2 I find who could be useful contacts	**1** I worry whether I will be able to fit in	**1** I act as myself

Now try the inventory yourself. Think of how you did or would behave in a similar situation and remember that nobody is looking over your shoulder – if possible think of how you actually behaved and not how you *should* have behaved with the 20:20 vision of hindsight.

SITUATION 1

When I am enjoying myself at work:

☐ Things are being done properly	☐ I am being of use to others	☐ My world is ordered, clear, and sensible
☐ I am being creative	☐ My world is warm and comfortable	☐ Nobody is holding back and I have time to breathe

SITUATION 2

When I am not getting what I want from other people:

☐ I push them harder	☐ I concern myself that they are getting it wrong	☐ I redefine the problem and seek a compromise
☐ I either move the goalposts or find a scapegoat	☐ I either blame myself or get angry	☐ I am inclined to lose interest and do something else

SITUATION 3

When I interview a candidate for a job:

☐ I look for people with the right attitudes	☐ I try to be helpful to the candidates	☐ I rely heavily on known facts and check what is on the form
☐ I work by intuition	☐ I abide by the rules picking people who fit in	☐ I either warm to people or not

SITUATION 4

When I feel I am being imposed upon:

☐ I claim my rights

☐ I take it as a compliment that they need me

☐ I set priorities and negotiate

☐ I make myself indispensable and go for terms

☐ I either get angry and bitter or go along with it

☐ I may well 'kick the cat' and think 'what the hell'

SITUATION 5

When I join a new team:

☐ I check out that things are being done properly

☐ I hope I can be of help

☐ I check out that the styles of working are appropriate

☐ I work out how it is structured – who is influential? is it going to work?

☐ I expect history to repeat itself

☐ I rather look forward to it – new people, new challenges

SITUATION 6

When I get direct opposition from an individual:

☐ I roll up my sleeves and fight

☐ I see the other's point of view and attempt to restore harmony

☐ I weigh the case and decide the best course of action

☐ I wish them luck and make sure they don't get it

☐ I can get mad or I can give in or I can settle myself down to a losing battle

☐ I put out my tongue at least proverbially and leave them to it

SITUATION 7

When I feel really good about myself:

☐ Others are turning to me for leadership and guidance

☐ I can see how my efforts are helping others

☐ I am into a really challenging problem

☐ I've pulled off what they said was impossible

☐ I feel respected and accepted

☐ The sun is shining and the breeze is blowing and I'm out there enjoying it

SITUATION 8

When I feel I cannot trust someone:

☐ I regret the betrayal

☐ I am saddened

☐ I analyse what happened and attempt to avoid any repetition

☐ I make sure they don't catch me again   ☐ I feel it was one of life's disappointments   ☐ '. . . well you win some and you lose some'

SITUATION 9
When I leave a place I would like to be remembered as:

☐ Someone who was respected   ☐ A person whom you could rely on for help   ☐ Sound and logical

☐ The person who could fix things   ☐ A good person   ☐ Fun to be with

SITUATION 10
When I feel I am being pressurised:

☐ I can get very aggressive   ☐ I try to be helpful   ☐ I prioritise and act appropriately

☐ I see it as an opportunity – 'they need me'   ☐ I do my best to resist but probably give in with good or bad grace   ☐ I walk out

The Inventory you have completed is based on the ideas of Eric Berne and provides a way of looking at the balance of States of Mind for individuals. By knowing our present state of mind one can hope to understand our behaviour at that time.

> Eric Berne recognised that there are three overall classifications for the *states of mind* of human beings. The clinical psychology of his day used language outside and away from an everyday context, and so Berne called his 'States of Mind' Parent, Adult and Child. Berne's use of these words to classify the states of mind of his patients is parallel, not identical, to the way we use them in everyday life. Even so, the words can be used to discuss human communication between ordinary healthy people.
>
> *The New Manager*, Element Books, 1988

The Parent state of mind produces behaviours learnt from the parents and the parent figures of one's childhood and we can almost imagine a little person saying to itself:

> 'I must remember how Daddy/Mummy handled that situation and use it when I am a big person and it happens again.'

The little person is completely dependent on big people and

SCORING:

Imagine the six boxes are thus:

A	B	C
D	E	F

Total your scores

	A	B	C	D	E	F		A	B	C	D	E	F
Statement 1							Statement 2						
Statement 3							Statement 4						
Statement 5							Statement 6						
Statement 7							Statement 8						
Statement 9							Statement 10						
TOTAL X							TOTAL Y						

obviously from the little person's perspective, big people are successful in coping with the complexities of the world, so copying big people is a sensible strategy. The problems may come when the 'little person' has grown up and still finds him or herself copying the behaviour of others from the past.

'As a parent I found the claim that my children were copying my behaviour, be it good, bad or awful as being both unlikely and frightening. That Berne was correct came to me when I watched my children giving a tea party for their Action Men. The 3-year-old turned on one of the dolls and stood arms pressed to hips and said: 'If you don't finish your dinner, you won't get any ice cream.'

It was as if it was me that was saying it, gestures, intonation, everything. Thinking on these lines I can find myself echoing things I heard my parents say. I was brought up during the times of World War shortages and a message in my head tells me that wasting food is bad and that is what I'm passing on – it's as if my parents are still telling me that I must not waste food and neither must my kids. There are lots of things like that – echoes of the past.'

Berne would see the ways of behaving that the little person files away for further use can come from two sub-sets of the Parent state of mind, one that copes critically with situations and another that copes with them in a nurturing or protective way.

> Our Parent state of mind has two parts –
> Critical parent and Nurturing Parent.

When the manager's child was standing arms to hips and instructing the Action Man to eat its toy plastic food, the little person was imitating his parents' critical behaviour and was acting in what Berne would call a Critical Parent State of Mind. The response to wasted food which would normally push the child's father into a critical state of mind had been passed on to the next generation. In a similar way, the child might have seen one of his friends fall over and hurt himself and copied a more caring reaction from his father or mother. A situation involving taking care of other people is inclined to make big people act from Nurturing Parent and the little person, the observant blotting paper, will copy. As a man or woman the 'grown up' little person is likely to continue to respond or at least want to respond to similar situations in the same way, however inappropriate the actual response is at the time. The Parent behaviours can be 'knee jerk' reactions to situations we perceive as similar to those of our childhood. The reactions are blind to the world that is now and are only responses to the distorted images of the past.

Legend has it that Berne did not find the name Child for his second state of mind easily and that he got his inspiration from a solicitor client who was riding Western saddle on a dude ranch.

When he approached the client formally he was told th[ ]
not talking to a solicitor but 'a little boy' – and so arose [ ]
state of mind.

The Child state of mind has three parts. The first is the Natural Child, who simply goes on doing things blissfully unaware of the world about it, the state presumably of the dude cow*boy*. The Natural Child state is emotional, selfish and fun and it is not 'customised' to the outside world. The 'customised' states are the two parts of the Adapted Child – 'Yes Sir' and 'I won't'. The 'Yes Sir' compliant Adapted Child reacts to the Parents' world about it by accepting what is happening. It is passive and knows how to please, be it by clowning or touching a forelock. The 'I won't' rebellious Adapted Child has had enough and says NO to everything and everyone just to annoy, but both the Adapted Child states are also *responses*, and are just as much 'knee jerks' as the Parent behaviours. Whereas the Parent responses are to part remembered events, the Child responses are responses to the Parent figures of the past.

> I was working with a group of Head Teachers and developing the concepts of Parent, Adult and Child. One of the teachers quite suddenly understood:
> 'That explains what happens when I tell kids off. Sometimes they do exactly as I want, sometimes they cry, sometimes they duck, sometimes they get defiant and other times they threaten the law. I always think I am doing the same. What you are saying is that I may be doing the same and that that is not relevant. They are not responding to *me* at all but to a heavy-handed Dad . . . someone from the past.'

Yes, that is what we are saying – the behaviour the Head Teacher got then depended on the little person's programming of the past.

We can imagine the baby in the womb soon learning that certain types of kicking make Mummy's tummy acid and that is uncomfortable for the unborn little person and therefore kicking is to be limited. The unborn Child is adapting for its own comfort – that is the compliant little person in front of the Head Teacher. However, under certain circumstances the unborn child may well carry on kicking just for the sake of it and to hell with the consequences. It could then be said to be punishing itself and Mummy – it is Rebelling. It is the little person in front of the Head Teacher who could be described as defiant.

Once the baby is born, the adapting process becomes much

more obvious. The initial skills in finding and getting Mummy's milk could well be instinctive but certainly the more sophisticated behaviours of gurgling for attention are learnt and come in response to what 'the big people' do. Big people seem to want a gurgling baby so the baby gurgles and is rewarded. The Nurturing Parent state of mind in Aunty Liz scratches little Fred's tummy when he gurgles, so he gurgles when he wants to have his tummy scratched. As a big person Fred will still try to get caring attention by something approaching gurgling. The move from gurgling as a response to gurgling as a form of manipulation is a massive development for the baby and Berne saw it as the birth of Adult behaviour in the little person. He called the nascent Adult in the little person Little Professor – the little person who in front of the Head Teacher had worked out the angles and was going to call in the law. All these sub-sets of the Child state of mind – Natural, Adapted (Acceptant/Rebellious) and Little Professor – are, as the Parent states, blind to the present.

> The scene is a supermarket and you have a little person tucked into the trolley. You have been a little over-enthusiastic with your purchases and you are hoping that the cheque/credit card limit you have agreed with the supermarket control desk is adequate to pay for your bulging trolley. As you come to the check-out, the last thing you want is a scene. You are under pressure. The little person with his or her legs stuffed through the wire of the basket has two choices:
>
> The first choice is to accept that Mummy or Daddy is under pressure and be quiet – to act in Adapted Child. The second choice is to understand that Mummy or Daddy is under pressure and exploit the situation. In this case the little person will recognise that there are goodies at the check-out and demand them – the Little Professor strikes again. Very few parents or guardians are in a good position to resist the blackmail of a potentially screaming youngster at a check-out for the price of a tube of sweets, and the little person – the Little Professor – knows it.

There are *two* Little Professors at the check-out – the little person with his or her legs through the wire of the supermarket trolley, and the designer of the supermarket. The designer of the supermarket put the goodies at the check-out knowing that you would be under pressure and would be less likely to resist blackmail.

Nobody and certainly not effective healthy human beings, could function with only Parent or Child states of mind. Such people would be restricted to acting from memories of the past –

copying past behaviour or reacting as they learnt to react to past behaviour. There has to be a state of mind that notices what is happening *now* and weighs matters – the Adult state of mind.

------▶

EXERCISE

Imagine you are visiting the factory of a customer and that you do not know the town. You have plenty of time and are organised enough to have a street map but you are held up in the main street by a student demonstration and finally arrive about five minutes late and rather hot and bothered. You give your name to the receptionist and pull yourself together. You ask directions to the toilet, have a cold douche and allow yourself to breathe steadily for a few minutes and then in the meeting apologise for being what is now ten minutes late. You begin your business.

If we think through the incident in terms of our states of mind at each stage we realise just how complex things are – try to voice the words that could be going through your head at each stage.

------▶

Talking to one manager working through this exercise, she explained that she always found strange towns a problem and that having to work from a map always made her feel very insecure – she saw herself clearly as being in Adapted Child and could hear herself saying – 'I hope this is the right road . . .'. 'Oh dear, it's a One Way . . .' – almost as if to an authority figure in the passenger seat. On one occasion she told us of when she rebelled and deliberately drove up a one-way street 'just to show them' – and she was not stopped by the police but did enjoy shouting back to helpful pedestrians who informed her of her error. On the issue of the students and the delays their demonstration caused, she could hear herself saying – 'They *should not* be holding up people like this . . . I pay for their grants.' – very Critical Parent indeed. The lateness would have put her back into Adapted Child – keeping the big people in her early life waiting was definitely not encouraged and she would find herself saying a lot of 'Sorry' when she was even a few minutes late. When she came to the reception desk she realised that the panic she found herself in would certainly not let her give a good presentation. Her Adult state of mind came to the rescue and she went to the washroom mainly to get herself centred and quietened so that she could perform effectively.

It is possible to recognise your own current state of mind by recognising how you are thinking about other people, how you are feeling and how you are behaving.

———————▶

EXERCISE

Imagine the situation where you have a reservation for a train and arrive exactly at the appointed time and find the train has just left. Our reactions are by no means definitive and the reader may like to insert his own particular versions.

Critical Parent	thinks –	'*They* have made a mistake.'
	feels –	aggrieved from superiority
	acts –	from superiority, is aggressive and could be seen as a persecutor
Nurturing Parent	thinks –	'I wonder if I can help anyone – they might not be able to afford a taxi/speak English/know the time of the next train.'
	feels –	superior
	acts –	helpfully, condescending, rescuing
Adult	thinks –	'Let's find out what happened before acting.'
	feels –	isolated but controlled
	acts –	appropriately
Little Professor	thinks –	'There's a thing!'
	feels –	excited
	acts –	in a manipulating way
Adapted Child	thinks –	'Oh dear . . .'
	feels –	inferior, impotent (*ME again!*)
	acts –	dependent or uselessly angry (to subordinates and not superintendents)
Natural Child	thinks –	'Damn . . . what the hell.'
	feels –	surprised but somehow released
	acts –	as the mood takes

ISSUES OF BEHAVIOUR

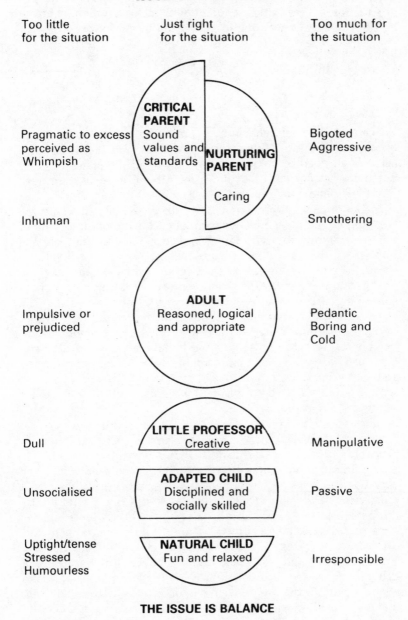

| Too little for the situation | Just right for the situation | Too much for the situation |

CRITICAL PARENT Sound values and standards

NURTURING PARENT Caring

Pragmatic to excess perceived as Whimpish — Bigoted Aggressive

Inhuman — Smothering

ADULT Reasoned, logical and appropriate

Impulsive or prejudiced — Pedantic Boring and Cold

LITTLE PROFESSOR Creative

Dull — Manipulative

ADAPTED CHILD Disciplined and socially skilled

Unsocialised — Passive

NATURAL CHILD Fun and relaxed

Uptight/tense Stressed Humourless — Irresponsible

THE ISSUE IS BALANCE

What would have been your predominant state of mind for the train incident? – what would you have thought, felt and actually done? How would your answers be changed by specific changes in situation – very critical appointment missed, previous errors by staff, not really wanting to get on the train anyway . . .

→

We can describe our behaviour as coming from three sets of states of mind and these influence how we think and hence how we act. We all need to be able to function in all the states of mind but there is good and bad news for others in all of them (see 'Issues of Behaviour', page 25).

In our own environment we are likely to have the relevant balance *and* the most effective form of each state of mind. Out of our own favoured environment and in situations that force us into stress, this is no longer true. Let's go back to the inventory we asked you to complete at the beginning of the chapter.

The X and Y scores for our inventory are designed to show something of the balance of the energy we spend in each of the states of mind, unstressed and stressed. For example, if we go back to the 'train incident' we suspect that every reader would be able to predict how they would behave on a 'good day' and on a 'bad day' given a similar incident. We have certain preferred states of mind and are recognised by others for them.

This is Betty's X score on our Inventory – the X score is for Betty on a good day.

Betty has a high Little Professor and Adult score. Her Natural Child is probably high for a manager and her Critical Parent is probably low but her Nurturing Parent is very low.

Working for Betty could be very exciting. You would find her very open to reasoned argument (high Adult) but rather manipulative in her dealings (high Little Professor). She would not be the person to go to for support (low Nurturing Parent) but her department could be great fun (Natural Child). The problem you could have working with Betty could well come from the low Critical Parent and Adapted Child. The Critical Parent in a manager is needed to set standards, define boundaries and take responsibility. If the profile we have for Betty is correct it is likely that she will allow *you* to define your own boundaries and allocate blame should you get it wrong and she is in the firing line. She

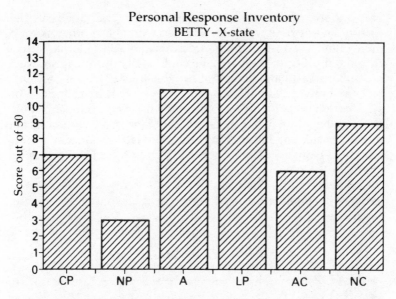

Personal Response Inventory
BETTY – X-state

will protect herself from Little Professor. The low Adapted Child may well mean that she has conflicts with her own bosses – she does not adapt 'naturally' to authority.

Now let's look at Betty's Y score – her pattern of energy in her states of mind on a bad day when she is being directly opposed, finds that she cannot trust others . . .

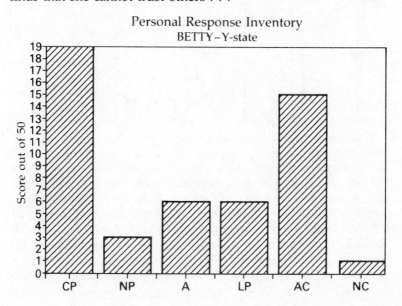

Personal Response Inventory
BETTY – Y-state

The pattern of energy is completely different. Suddenly her
Critical Parent rises with her Adapted Child. The other states of
mind almost vanish. Under pressure she will lose her strong
Adult and act from the past. She could well appear aggressive to
her subordinates and acceptant or rebellious to her bosses. On a
bad day Betty could well be a person to keep away from. It is the
switch from the X to the Y profile that will give us problems. Betty
could move from what at worst could be seen as a cold and
selfish, calculating but exciting and stimulating manager – to the
moody personality. The switch will give her and her colleagues
grief.

Campbell is different again. With his X score we can recognise
many of the points from his description of his fondly remembered
experience.

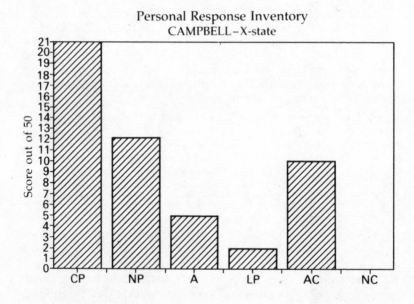

Personal Response Inventory
CAMPBELL – X-state

In the experience he discussed his strong sense of values (high
Critical Parent) and clear objectives. He showed himself to be a
strong leader who might well have given up an 'impossible task'
had he been 'sensible' (Adult). He was loyal to management and
his own bosses, and he really cared about the way his staff felt
about him (Adapted Child and Nurturing Parent). How about
Campbell on a bad day – his Y scores?

Campbell on a bad day moves his energies strongly into

Nurturing Parent and away from Adapted Child. He also gains in Little Professor and drops his Critical Parent.

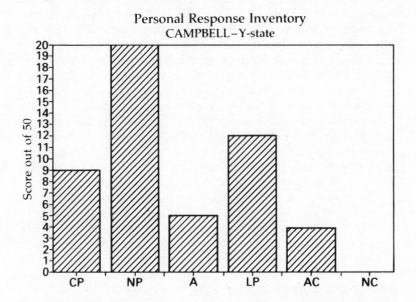

Personal Response Inventory
CAMPBELL – Y-state

The behaviour that Campbell now could display is illustrated by his own account of why he had to leave his previous company.

He was a production manager when the company was in trouble. He had managed to get his team working effectively but was called in to the boardroom and told that he had to lose 30 per cent by forced redundancy. In what was seen as a completely uncharacteristic manner, he opposed the Managing Director face to face and finally was forced to resign after he had released the story to a local reporter.

The movement from the X to the Y patterns of energy distribution may give rise to further problems in that the Y (stressed) balance of states of mind may not give rise to the same quality of behaviour. The behaviours coming from each of the states of mind in the X (unstressed) balance could well be concerned with our valued skills and be from our 'Just Right' column – Sound Values and Standards from Critical Parent, Caring about others from Nurturing Parent, Reasoned and Appropriate behaviour from our Adult and Creative, Disciplined and Relaxed behaviour from our Child. They are likely to be balanced and perceived as appropriate by others because they have been subjected to the feedback of approval and disapproval for all our years on earth. The Y (stressed) balance of states of mind could well lead to a less effective set of behaviours – aggression or bigotry from an increased contribution from Critical Parent or perhaps a smothering 'mother hen' from increased Nurturing Parent. The Y scores may well produce behaviour not so finely honed by feedback.

For most of us the 'normal state balance' of X scores has had time to become adapted as a whole to the world around us and we have adapted the world to fit it. The Y score world is not how we like it and no process of compromise has had time to occur. An example of a movement from the X balance to the Y balance was that which produced inappropriate behaviour in Campbell and his forced resignation. Campbell increased his Nurturing Parent to the extent of being uncontrolled under pressure. His Adult was not available to correct and his Adapted Child to produce sufficient 'respect' to allow him to negotiate some settlement which would have allowed him to stay and *help* his workers rather than martyring himself over them. There is a footnote to our X and Y scores. We have attempted to make a judgement on what situations cause stress in managers – you may like to review the situation in both the X and Y set and adapt them to situations *you* find 'good' or 'stressed'.

---------➤

EXERCISE

Review your own X and Y scores – if possible discuss them with a colleague:

1   Does the X score reflect your 'normal' style of management? Are there any problems you can see from the profile – a high Nurturing Parent may well mean that you are treated as a Social Worker by your staff and find it hard to be taught, a high Adult may make you *too* reasonable, a low Adapted Child may put you in conflict with your own bosses.

2   Compare balances of states of mind from the X and Y scores.

	GOOD news	BAD news
If nothing changes	level/calm style	flat and unresponsive
Rise in Critical P	tougher/directive	may be inappropriate
Fall in Critical P	more pragmatic	fall in standards
Rise in Nurturing P	more caring	'mother hen'
Fall in Nurturing P	sense of proportion	callous
Rise in Adult	common sense	isolation
Fall in Adult	more human	unconsidered actions
Rise in LP	calculated action	self-centred slyness
Fall in LP	genuine	stupid responses
Rise in Adapted C	more sensible	whimpish or rebel
Fall in Adapted C	assertive	suicidal actions
Rise in Natural C	personal survival	loss of respect and care
Fall in Natural C	concern	stress

How does your change of balance of states of mind, if there is one, affect you, your team, your peers and your bosses?

In the next chapter we are going to look at how the process of:

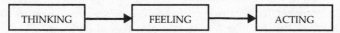

can get out of hand and lead us into a Catastrophe Spiral. The Catastrophe Spiral happens when the thinking coming from the echoes of the past leads us to feel inappropriately to those around us and act in a less than productive way. The unproductive behaviour may then be reinforced by what subsequently happens. Others, perceiving our 'attitude' and not having the skills, aptitude or inclination to find out what is going on in our heads, may well push us in a way that makes us act even more inappropriately – for instance in our earlier example of the ticket collector – if we started from a feeling of superiority and acted aggressively, the ticket inspector might well resent our behaviour and tell us so. We, as a result of this 'telling off' might get even more aggressive and . . . This is the Catastrophe Spiral and it has caused many of us to falter, if not fall.

CHAPTER THREE

Mind Music, or 'I have often been down this street before'

'I know, I know, I have been told dozens of times, but it's like a trigger.'

'I simply have to say No, but always I find myself arguing.'

'It's either win or lose with me, and recently its been more lose than win.'

'I THINK, THEREFORE I FEEL, THEREFORE I ACT.'

'I seem to have been doing this sort of thing all my life.' I was talking to Dennis, a junior executive of a large multi-national and he was telling me of a recent incident.

Dennis, the Marketing Vice-President, had been away from the office for a few days and had decided to come in early and tackle his desk before the inevitable rush of phone calls and visitors. He had hardly settled down to open his first file when the phone rang. It was the Chief Executive's secretary who was 'very glad to have caught him'.

'Could you come up straight away, he says it's very urgent.'

Before Dennis was even in the lift, he had reviewed all the things that he might have done wrong in the last week, and by the time he was facing his boss across the leather-topped desk, the whole situation had made him feel more like a schoolboy facing the Head Teacher than a Marketing Vice-President – he was definitely in Adapted Child.

'Got this letter from Malaysia this morning.' The letter was thrust forward for him to keep. 'The last batch was all wrong – get out there by Friday and see what's happened – no – send Higgins, she'll know. OK? Yes *now*.'

The interview had not reassured Dennis and it was as a very small boy escaping from the Head Teacher that he virtually ran out of the office and down the stairs. he was still running when he bumped into Higgins on her way to the computer suite. Out of breath, he ordered Higgins into his own office and passed his instructions on to her. Higgins, being a very reasonable human being and well in control of herself, attempted to explain that going to Malaysia by Friday would help nobody. It would take all of that day to sort out the batch numbers and the samples could not be tested in less than twenty-four hours, and today was Wednesday. Dennis then got nasty and the meeting ended with Higgins planning a revenge on Dennis, with whom her relations had previously been excellent. She bought Executive Class air tickets for herself and two of her department and arranged directly with the customer to arrive the *next* Friday with a jet-lag stop-over in Hong Kong. Higgins was quite aware that Dennis, a mere Vice-President, would be unable to authorise any of these things without referral to the Chief Executive.

We were told of the incident some weeks after the event and the immediate issues had already been sorted out. Higgins had compromised and only taken one assistant and the stop-over had been cancelled. The company had been persuaded that the executive class travel on this occasion was justified but Dennis was still far from happy. Even after the intervening weeks he felt confused, angry and anxious with his personal issues unresolved. He put it quite simply:

I find myself in this sort of situation over and over again. The point for me is that I expect people to act reasonably. I do not expect the Chief Executive to issue unconsidered orders – he is paid a lot not to. Why didn't I question him at the time? Why didn't I question him or my previous boss on previous occasions? Higgins? Higgins is paid well and ought to act responsibly, but when she questioned me – reasonably as I saw within seconds of sitting down – I just got into a shouting match. I do the same thing with my kids. It's like getting into a sort of catastrophe spiral. I get angry, they don't kowtow and I get more angry.

For me the result is always the same, I go home by way of the pub and feel lousy and the slightest thing sends me into real anger. Over and over again I finish having to tidy . . . to clean up after things like that. Sometimes I think the ideal place for me is to be on a desert island or a company completely run by computers.

———————▶

EXERCISE

Firstly think in terms of the movement of Dennis in the X (unstressed) balance of states of mind to the Y (stressed) balance.

What happened?

Secondly, read over the two parts of the Dennis case history and think in terms of the messages that he was hearing in his own head at the various critical points in what ended as a very difficult situation.

For instance when he arrived in early to get his desk cleared it is quite possible that he was congratulating himself on 'being a good boy'.

How did the messages in his head – we shall call them *mind music* – change when the secretary rang him and again, how did they change on his way to the Chief Executive's office?

What mind music was he hearing when he agreed to the impossible task and how did the theme change when he found himself unreasonably pressurising Higgins?

                                                              ———————▶

From the second chapter we can probably put words to what happened to Dennis and how he got into his *catastrophe spiral*. 'On a good day' Dennis was a strong and logical manager – high in Adult – but under pressure his Y balance showed quite a movement – from Adult into Adapted Child and Critical Parent. The Adapted Child was what met the Boss – 'Yes sir, no sir, three bags full sir.'

It was Dennis acting from his Critical Parent state of mind that met Higgins – his subordinate: 'Higgins is paid well and ought to act responsibly.'

The problem with Dennis is that once he had found himself in Adapted Child with his boss things seemed to get worse. He found himself in the Adapted Child state of mind originally by feeling as he had done when he visited the Head Teacher's study in the past. These feelings he had translated to the present and prevented any possibility of an Adult conversation:

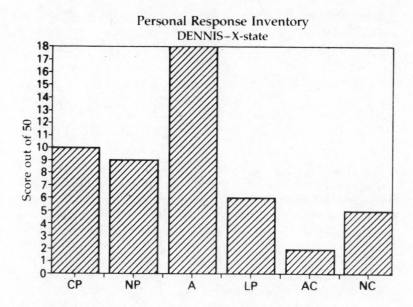

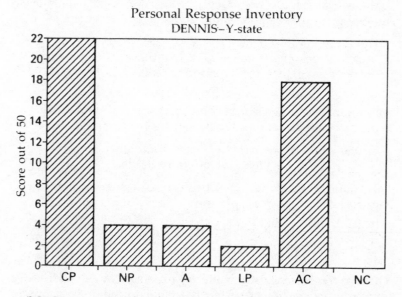

'Mr Green says you were caught smoking in the games room.'
Sorry sir. It won't happen again sir . . .'

A lot of thoughts were going through Dennis' head when he met the Chief Executive and these thoughts disempowered Denis the man. The boss, who was in reality a reasonable person, found a wimpish subordinate standing in front of him and treated him accordingly.

> If you behave as a wimp, people will treat you as a wimp, and it is very difficult not to act even more wimpishly – rebellious or compliant – and the spiral begins.

The person who invites bullying as a child often invites bullying for the rest of their lives.

With Jean Higgins the thoughts in Dennis' head also blocked any appropriate action. He thought of himself as the authority figure and felt and acted in that way towards her – without any consideration that such behaviour, in the total environment that existed at the time, was less than productive. Where he should have called for serious discussion and advice, he bullied. By acting aggressively towards Higgins he was demanding that she adopt an Adapted Child state of mind and the more she refused his demands and remained as logical Adult, the more the messages in his head – the mind music – told him that 'she ought to do as I say' and he increased the pressure. Finally she moved her energy into Rebellious Child and she 'got her revenge'.

> The thoughts in our heads – *mind music* – are triggered by situations echoing from the past that make us feel 'inferior' – Adapted Child – or 'superior' – Critical Parent to those around us.

> If others encourage our belief – reinforce our mind music – we remain in our chosen states of mind.

> If others refuse to accept the states of mind we have chosen for them, we often try harder.

> The mind music may well become so deafening that any possibility of rational appropriate behaviour is impossible.

> If we do not review the relevance of our approach we may well get into some excess of behaviour – the catastrophe spiral.

This chapter is concerned with the processes by which we can gain a temporary silence from the mind music and review its relevance to the present. We will attempt to codify the beliefs that provide the themes of the music and develop certain simple techniques that allow us our moment of silence to review the real world and decide, undeafened by the mind music, what is an appropriate action for us at this moment in our lives. Unsilenced, the mind music leads us to move virtually as a knee-jerk response into a locked Nurturing Parent, Critical Parent, Adult or Adapted Child state of mind.

The Mind Music

'Why cannot a woman be more like a man?'

To act effectively we need to act appropriately, and this is particularly difficult in situations we find personally stressful. In personally stressful situations it is as if our mind music – messages coming from the past – deafens us to the present and compels us into restricted patterns of behaviour.

The mind music makes us *think* a particular way.	We consequently *feel* in a set way to people and circumstances	and we *act* in a set way.

For example we may find that some things and some people always 'make us furious' and if we listen dispassionately to ourselves we can hear a chunner of messages from the past saying things like 'they *ought* not to do that . . .', 'sensible people don't behave in that way . . .' The inappropriate behaviour that the mind music produces is always debilitating and disempowering in some way:

> Boris Becker, 1986 Wimbledon Tennis Men's Singles Champion was defeated in the 1987 Championship by a relatively unknown player – Peter Doohan. Obviously appropriate behaviour in the Wimbledon Tennis Championship is 'going in there and winning', but in an interview with the *Guardian* newspaper the next day he confided:

> 'I kept thinking he would crack and I would win easily, I kept saying that he is not a Lendl or Leconte and I thought he could not play the four sets as he did.'

The mind music in Becker's head was telling him that Doohan as a much less renowned player would 'let' him win and he, Becker, did not have to try so hard. The mind music is often a betrayer, at best echoing what could be the relevant past. We are not all Beckers but we all have mind music which, at times, compels us, if we let it, into inappropriate anger, inappropriate caring or inappropriate subservient activity. Anger, caring or subservience may or may not be the correct response for the particular situation that faces us, but the compulsion towards these behaviours created by listening to the archaic mind music always needs to be reviewed. Behaviour needs to be relevant to be effective and not as a 'knee-jerk' to situations resembling half-remembered scenes of the past. The compulsion of anger, or of any other response to a set of circumstances debilitates us and, as in the case of Becker, may persuade us to depend on outside factors to do our work for us. Becker felt that he did not have to play so well because his opponent's mistakes would win for him. Our inability to be master of our own responses makes us less effective as human beings.

The review and if necessary the censorship of the commands of our mind music allows us the opportunity of real personal development. To undertake the beginning of such a personal development we need first to understand something of our own mind music and then to find out how to 'buy time' so that we can review the content of the messages dispassionately in the framework of our real lives at the present moment in time. The mind music can be orchestrated into a number of themes or belief systems which make us think about how things *ought* to be – how Becker thought his opponent *ought* to play tennis, how Dennis thought his boss *ought* to have 'thought things through' or how he thought Jean Higgins *should* have shown him respect as her boss.

Albert Ellis, a respected psychologist, codified four belief systems he considered caused 'nine-tenths of all human suffering':

Belief System 1: An overall purpose for the Universe

'GOD WOULDN'T LET THIS HAPPEN.'

'IT WILL BE ALL RIGHT ON THE NIGHT.'

The belief is that of an overall cosmic order of things extending to individual problems. We are not saying that the religions of the world are wrong. We are only calling into question the personal responsibility of a cosmic entity for local issues. We are saying that a belief that 'God owes *me* a living because I have done certain things' is open to question. The greatest of us can share such belief systems and Einstein for instance believed in the 'simplicity' of the divine order and presented what seemed to be a closed mind to the more complex solutions opened by Heisenburg and others.

Belief System 2: A fundamental belief in hierarchy

'THE COMPANY WILL PROTECT ME.'

'THE BOSS KNOWS BEST.'

The belief is concerned with order and Galbraith discusses it in terms of 'taking on a great man's garment'. Somehow we believe that because people have some sort of superior status or role, they are superior in all ways. We believe that on promotion a manager *assumes* more significance and we ignore the more likely scenario that having more responsibility forces one to work harder and longer and thus be inclined to make more mistakes. We may also believe the corollary – because people do not have status in a specific area, they are inferior in all other ways.

John Stalker, ex-Assistant Chief Constable of Greater Manchester Police in England explained that one of his great problems was accepting that he owed deference to the uniform but not to the man. Others have the same problem.

Belief System 3: Others should behave to our standards or beliefs

The belief is somehow concerned with the issue of others sharing our mind music. If we feel compelled to help an old person across the road, whether they want to cross or not, *they* somehow have to be grateful. If we are working hard/late hours to set standards, others *should* as well, without any discussion or negotiation.

As part of a large conglomerate an engineering group was heading for closure and the current board decided on a management buyout. After two years, and a considerable amount of 'midnight oil equity' the company had been turned round to a glowing and profitable success. The 'midnight oil equity' had meant 60 to 100 hours a week working but the new owners considered it worth it. Unfortunately at the end of the two-year period the managers had got into the habit of living at the workplace *and* expecting everyone else to do the same.

'I have simply lost the habit of normal office hours and obviously expect the support staff to be around when I want them.'

And much worse:

'I expect them to have the same commitment and I feel they should have; I know it's silly. I get really hostile if they talk about 'going home to help bath the kids'.

Belief System 4: I must behave in a prescribed way to be a good person

'TO BE A FULL PERSON I MUST:

– PASS EXAMS
– BE A GOOD WIFE
– BE A SUCCESSFUL PARENT.'

Belief System 4 is a curse we may well have inherited from well-meaning parents. The good life is somehow conditional on passing certain hurdles. If you do not conform to standards, jump these hurdles, you have somehow failed, not just as standard attainer or hurdle jumper, but as a human being. The failure is not simply in the performance but in your existence – to fail an exam is to deprive you of love in your parents' eyes.

Taibi Kahler split the Ellis Belief Systems into what she called Drivers. These Drivers she acknowledges have no theoretical basis but simply fitted the Parent and Adapted Child messages she found in the people she worked with. We can imagine the Drivers as being the sub-themes of our personal mind music. We hear the sub-themes played in our ears as we move through patterns of half-remembered experiences of childhood.

'Go on hurry up – they will all be gone . . .'

'It's got to be *right* – it's got to be perfect – no mistakes are allowed . . .'

'Keep at it. Show them by working hard, try harder.'

'Big boys don't cry. Show them. Be strong.'

'Go on give them a hand – just to please me.'

Working with managers who wish to go beyond the scope of this book, and actually challenge their mind music, it is surprising how the actual words they feel they can hear in their heads seem to have a commonality.

Kahler gave the individual Drivers – our sub-themes – the titles:

Hurry Up
Be Perfect
Try Hard
Be Strong
Please Me

The examples of the sub-themes of the mind music in our heads from the various Drivers produced could be:

Driver	Theme of thoughts on your own personal stereo:	
	about YOURSELF	about OTHERS
HURRY UP	I ought to be able to do everything *now*, even if it means without planning or even thinking	If I am in a hurry so should others be or they are *wrong*
BE PERFECT	Mistakes are never acceptable and people who make mistakes are inferior	Proper people should comply to our standards
TRY HARD	It is important to put your back into it	Hard work is a sign of goodness
BE STRONG	Pull yourself together – there is no way they will see any weakness	Letting themselves down by showing emotion – 'pull yourself together'
PLEASE ME	You have a duty to help others *always*	Others should be grateful

Organisations as well as individuals seem to have Mind Music and particular belief systems. In some organisations – such as the Police – it is not acceptable to show any personal weakness (Be Strong). In others, such as the organisation we mentioned in the management buyout, it was necessary to work gross overtime to be accepted (Try Hard). In less horrendous examples of organisations with a Try Hard sub-theme you may well feel 'dressed unfit for work' unless you are carrying a briefcase or a pile of computer output as you scurry between offices. Organisations may insist on the detail of clothing and presentation (Be Perfect) or work on the principle of crisis management (Hurry Up). Knowing your own Mind Music and comparing its themes with those of the organisation can help us to understand some of our conflicts at work.

EXERCISE

Consider the following scenario and decide what sort of belief systems might have caused the beginning of the catastrophe spiral.

MR EDWARDS AND THE FINANCE DIRECTOR

Mr Edwards was the departmental manager of a small manufacturing unit within a holding company, the other parts of the company being largely in the retail or service sector. Over the previous years he had had open and constructive discussions with the Finance Director on the presentation of the main accounts, Mr Edwards maintaining that the presentation of accounts was not ideal for a business operating in a high fixed cost arena.

At the formal presentation of the annual company accounts to all senior managers Mr Edwards noticed a small arithmetical error in the published profit and loss account. He pointed out the error in a helpful way at the meeting.

The response was not as he expected.

An obvious answer could be that Mr Edwards was working from a Be Perfect Driver and that he felt 'mistakes are a sign of slackness and/or inferiority' but this was not the main issue for Mr Edwards. Why did he operate in what was in fact a suicidal way and give 'advice' in public to a senior manager? Talking to him it was quite obvious he was 'trying to help' – he was listening to the Please Me theme from his personal mind music – and missing the reality of the situation. He genuinely thought that he was 'giving a hand' and advice was given in Adapted Child to what he saw as a respected Parent figure. The Finance Director unfortunately was not hearing the same mind music as Mr Edwards but was listening to themes in his own head saying that 'employees did not criticise their bosses in public' and that 'Edwards should know his place.' The Finance Director's beliefs at that time, unfortunately for Mr Edwards, were orchestrated on the Hierarchy theme. The Critical Parent that was picked up by the Finance Director was not part of Mr Edwards' make-up but he was still asked to resign.

Try the rest of the case studies.

EXERCISE

What belief systems were operating in the following case studies?

MRS FRANCIS GOES SHOPPING

Mrs Francis took her teenage daughter shopping to buy a new pair of jeans in a large shopping precinct. At the first shop she identified a perfectly satisfactory pair of jeans for her daughter but they were not quite as Miss Francis wanted – the style was no longer fashionable. Six shops later they had still not bought any jeans and Mrs Francis was beginning to lose patience and worry that they would miss their train home.

The existing situation is that Mrs and Miss Francis are communicating through notes passed through Miss Francis' younger brother.

GEORGE AND A JOB FOR LIFE

George had worked for Bloggs Bros. for twenty years. Although not spectacular in his progress, he was well-known for his reliability and tenacity. He arrived early in the mornings and was 'willing and hard-working', to quote his appraisal form. He had a strong respect for old Mr Bloggs and has long since accepted that the routes to promotion were by 'being family' or having been to the correct public school. George was not family and had not been to a public school, correct or otherwise.

Two days before Christmas he was made redundant and had a nervous breakdown.

MRS HARRISON AND THE YOUNGER WOMAN

Mrs Harrison was a devoted wife and mother – her family were her life. During the celebration of her silver wedding anniversary she learnt that her husband was about to leave her for a younger woman.

Mrs Harrison was distressed and brave but exploded when a neighbour offered her comfort with the words:

'Now you can build a new life for yourself.'

⟶

Looking at the case studies one at a time we may suspect that Mrs Francis could well be hearing Mind Music about the relative status of herself and her daughter. Her personal stereo is saying:

'She ought to be grateful . . .' It's not really her money anyway.' 'In my day a daughter knew her place.' – Belief System 2, about hierarchy.

Mrs Francis also displayed impatience and the Mind Music could well be:

'If she doesn't hurry up we will miss that train.' 'Go on, get on with it.' That will do . . . we haven't got all day.' – Hurry Up Driver.

None of these words may actually be said but they are what is being heard in Mrs Francis' head at the time.

Miss Francis may well be listening to a different set of themes from her personal Mind Music:

'Look, it's got to be *right*.' 'I need to know this is exactly what the others are wearing.' 'Those are fine but not *JUST* as I want them.' – Be Perfect Driver.

The more Mrs Francis allows herself to listen to her Hurry Up driver, the less she can hear from her daughter and understand the situation that is arising. Correspondingly Miss Francis, blocked from communication with her mother, becomes deafened by her own driver telling her to Be Perfect and both of them head into a Catastrophe Spiral.

In the second example the messages in George's head could be telling him the 'firm *owed* him for his long service' – other people ought to be grateful (Please Me). He will also be hearing messages in his head about loyalty and service. George has a set of beliefs in System 2 – hierarchy.

In the third example of Mrs Harrison we have a very full programme of mind music but unfortunately with different themes for her and her neighbour.

Mrs Harrison is on the System 2 Hierarchy/Please Me theme – 'I've been a good wife and it's not fair.' She sees herself as pleasing others all her life and she is owed gratitude (Please Me). She believes in the hierarchical structure of marriage and its responsibilities and 'it's not fair' that others feel otherwise. Whether we agree or disagree with Mrs Harrison is not the point – that is what she believes and that is the mind music in her head. The neighbour has different mind music relating to standing on one's own two feet (Be Strong). For her the way in which Mrs Harrison is taking it is *wrong*. Her advice is likely to be: 'Pull yourself together . . .' because she feels that people who do not pull themselves together and are not 'strong' about things are somehow inferior. Unfortunately Mrs Harrison's personal stereo is on a different station: she is listening to different music playing themes with no resemblance to those in her neighbour's head. Advice is often from our own personal mind music, without regard to what the other person is thinking – advice can often be worthless.

Mind Music is perfectly capable of blocking out Adult and relevant thinking for a particular situation.

Once this blocking has occurred, potentially inappropriate action is virtually inevitable.

The issue is that of being able to review the noise in your head and decide what is relevant and what is rubbish. For that we need time.

➤

EXERCISE

Think of at least six situations where you found yourself not performing as you would have liked.

Examples of two situations we have met in the past are of a professional having difficulties explaining technicalities to his or her seniors in formal conditions, perhaps in a boardroom, and of another effective manager having problems disciplining a subordinate in the situation where he felt the organisation was not being truly fair.

Take a definite example and decide what you were actually attempting to do.

Look back on your list and attempt to recall the mind music that was playing in your head at the time.

Were your actions at the time determined by your mind music or by your judgement of what was necessary?

——————————————▶

Doing this exercise, one manager recalled the following incident:

I was, up to this incident, regarded as a 'high flyer'. I was presenting a paper to the board on a special project – the result of some months work. I had circulated the report to the board with agenda in the previous week and was looking forward to some really good discussion. I was proud of the report and of the work. The report was given a good spot on the agenda but then things started to go wrong. I was getting really uninformed criticism from senior people who had obviously not even looked at the thing until they sat down – thumbing through and skip reading. I evidently showed some annoyance and I am told was very rude to the Finance Director.

The manager's Mind Music was concerned with the feeling of 'being a good boy' who deserved rewards for having done good work. He felt hostile to the Technical Director because the music in his head said that he 'had no right to criticise without having done his homework properly'. People are remarkably adept in recognising how others feel about them. In discussion the mind music went much further in that he felt 'anyone who was making that sort of money *ought* to know better.' As we said, he very nearly got fired on the spot –

> To behave effectively we need to have time to review the mind music in our heads against the actual situation and decide on relevant action – we must be able to give ourselves pause.

Going back to our example concerning Dennis, Higgins and the Malaysian customer, the conversations might have gone differently:

> 'Got this letter from Malaysia this morning. The last batch was all wrong – get out by Friday and see what's happening – no, send Higgins, she'll know.'

If we listen to the music in our heads saying that the Chief Executive is always right and that our views are not really in the same class, we will agree and the catastrophe spiral is primed.

WHY DO WE NOT BUY TIME
SO WE CAN REVIEW
THE MESSAGES IN OUR HEAD?

> 'May I have a few minutes to read the letter and get back to you? I need a short time to digest the contents.'

It's easy. Very few situations indeed need an immediate response.

RULE NUMBER 1.
WHEN YOU ARE UNDER PRESSURE – *BUY TIME.*

BUYING TIME CAN BE DIFFICULT, HOWEVER, IF THE OTHER PERSON WILL NOT RESPECT YOUR RIGHTS.

> 'Got this letter from Malaysia this morning. The last batch was all wrong – get out by Friday and see what's happening – no, send Higgins, she'll know.'

> 'May I have a few minutes to read the letter and get back to you? I need a short time to digest the contents.'

> 'Look, I don't think you heard me. I want it done *now.*'

> 'I would like a few minutes to read the letter and then I can get back to you.'

> 'Look Dennis, get on with it.'

> 'I still need a few minutes to read the letter.'

> 'Right, come back to me in ten minutes.'

Simply deciding on a position and redefining it *over* and *over* again does work. The technique of Broken Record, as it is known, is simple and does allow us time to review our position. It does allow us time to block out the mind music.

To resist pressure and buy time use:
BROKEN RECORD
Decide on a position
Use a level voice
Do not be afraid to say the same thing over and over again
Do not be drawn and remember you do not need to answer questions

In our example, the going may get harder and the Chief Executive may begin to vary the pressure. Dennis might also find that the pressure begins to be such that he feels he is about to be fired on the spot, and he has the choice of backing down.

'Got this letter from Malaysia this morning. The last batch was all wrong – get out by Friday and see what's happening – no, send Higgins, she'll know.'

'May I have a few minutes to read the letter and get back to you? I need a short time to digest the contents.'

'Look, I don't think you heard me. I want it done *now*.'

'I would like a few minutes to read the letter and then I can get back to you.'

'Look Dennis, get on with it.'

'I still need a few minutes to read the letter.'

'If we don't get this letter replied to immediately we are likely to lose a vital customer.'

'I understand that this is a concern. I still need a few minutes to sort things out.'

'Dennis this is really important – I need your response *now*.'

'I realise you would like an immediate response, but I still need some time to understand what has to be done.'

Reading the dialogue this time we can see that Dennis is acknowledging what the Chief Executive has to say – *but is still not budging from his prepared position*. He is using Fielding.

FIELDING – taking the sting out of pressure

Listen to what the other person says

Acknowledge that you have heard them,
using some of the same words

Accept that they have a right to their opinion

Accept the truth, however small, in what they say

Maintain your position by Broken Record

You do not have to defend, blame or justify

Stay with the technique – forget the mind music

Ultimately the Chief Executive will either throw you or Dennis out or begin to realise that you are not a wimp and actually are worth the money he or she is paying you. There has to be some form of compromise.

'I understand that this is a concern, I still need a few minutes to sort things out.'

'Dennis this is really important – I need a response *now*.'

'I realise you would like an immediate response, but I still need some time to understand what has to be done. Look, how about my sitting in the next office for a few minutes to digest what you are telling me and perhaps ringing Quality Control to find how long it will take to get the batch numbers. That will take about twenty minutes. I'll come right back then, OK?'

'You realise the importance – OK, twenty minutes, but no longer.'

We have a workable compromise.

WORKABLE COMPROMISE

When and only when you feel you have resisted
the pressure

Listen for clues
from the person putting you under pressure

Ask – What would they reasonably settle for that would not
undermine your position?

It must work for both of you

Timing is all-important – not too early or too late

Workable Compromises are not always possible

In the real world the problem we all meet is that, however much
we practise our skills, at some times we will have to deal with
people who have no acceptance of not *winning*. They are not used
to assertive people. If you stick to an assertive stance with such
people you are likely to be seen as dangerous, awkward and
worst perhaps of all – *someone who is to be avoided*. We know of no
solution to this except the use of the second Rule:

RULE NUMBER 2.
ASSERTIVE BEHAVIOUR IS *NOT* ABOUT GETTING YOUR
OWN WAY. ASSERTIVE BEHAVIOUR *IS* ABOUT BALANCE,
UNDERSTANDING AND CHOICE.

YOUR MIND MUSIC MAY WELL BE RIGHT!

ALLOW YOURSELF TIME TO THINK AGAIN ABOUT ALL
THE CONSEQUENCES IF THE GOING IS GETTING TOUGH.

EXERCISE

Complete the following dialogue using Broken Record, Fielding and Workable Compromise.

Boss: The situation is this – we need about 10 per cent reduction in manpower across the plant.

John: You mean my group has to take 10 per cent down on manpower?

Boss: I am afraid that is what I do mean. Can you give me a scheme by next Friday?

John: That's ridiculous. I am already stretched, any reduction is out of the question.

Boss: USE BROKEN RECORD

John: They must be mad.

Boss: USE FIELDING AND BROKEN RECORD

John: Look, don't they know what it's like in Production? No of course they don't. Too busy worrying out Marketing. No way.

Boss: FIELDING AND BROKEN RECORD

John: To hell with Marketing. I just cannot sort out 10 per cent by Friday.

Boss: EXPLORE FOR WORKABLE COMPROMISE – BEGIN WITH FIELDING

John: Well there are a lot of things to do. Could we meet again on the 22nd?

Boss: CLARIFY

John: I suppose so.

Boss: OK, 22nd first thing.

⟶

The dialogue might look like this:

Boss: The situation is this – we need about 10 per cent reduction in manpower across the plant.

John: You mean my group has to take 10 per cent down on manpower?

Boss: I am afraid that is what I do mean. Can you give me a scheme by next Friday?

John: That's ridiculous. I am already stretched, any reduction is out of the question.

Boss: I'm sorry John, I have to insist on 10 per cent.

John: They must be mad.

Boss: I know it may seem that way but I still need a plan for
        10 per cent reduction by Friday.

John: Look, don't they know what it's like in Production? No
        of course they don't. Too busy worrying out Marketing.
        No way.

Boss: I know it may seem that way, but at the end of the day
        we need 10 per cent from you. Even Marketing is
        having to bite the bullet.

John: To hell with Marketing. I just cannot sort out 10 per
        cent by Friday.

Boss: How long will it take?

John: Well there are a lot of things to do. Could we meet
        again on the 22nd?

Boss: We are talking about names and job specs – the lot?

John: I suppose so.

Boss: OK, 22nd first thing.

It may sound too easy – using the simple techniques of Broken
Record, Fielding and Workable Compromise and expecting ourselves to be allowed to behave appropriately – it is. All the
techniques do is allow us temporary respite from the pressures
of the mind music by buying time. Having bought that time, we
are likely to have reduced the pressure upon ourselves and be in
a position to work from full knowledge of the situation in front
of us *now* and act as effectively as possible. Even so we are only
talking about working with reasonable people who want to get
the job done. The issue of the next chapter is how to survive
against people who are trying to drive us into the ground –
people who know how to encourage our mind music for their
own good – the manipulators.

-->

'Sorry' is not a Word – it's a Life Sentence

'It's amazing, anybody, however humble, only has to criticise me and I look down at my proverbial zip (or stockings) – I feel guilty straight away and probably show it.'

Certain people seem to have a skill in being able to encourage our mind music in a way that helps them achieve their goals. These people are able to find our particular stressors and bring them to the fore, and very often they make us feel guilt in the process. We will begin this chapter by discussing the strategy these 'other people' may use to get us to do things for them – how they persuade us that *their* problem is somehow *our* problem. We will call people able to get us to do their jobs for them – 'task manipulators'. The previous chapter has told us how to deal with pressure assertively using Broken Record and Fielding, but in practice, the skilled manipulator knows how to deafen us with our own mind music *before* we quite know what we are being called upon to refuse assertively. We will explain two further techniques to reduce the chances of manipulators amplifying our mind music and provide a general strategy to deal with situations likely to give us pressure. Finally we will discuss the issue of people who wind us up for personal rather than 'professional' reasons – people who want us to *be* something to them. These we will call the 'role manipulators'.

We will begin with the 'task manipulators' – the people who simply want us to *do* things for them.

A problem shared is a problem halved, or if you are lucky – handed on.

The technique of the 'task manipulator' – consciously or by habit is to make the innocent rest of us accept the premise that we are in this world to help them. The sequence of operation is:

1   I have a problem.
2   You could solve my problem.
3   It is your duty to help me.
4   You can help me, therefore you will help me.
5   So now it's your problem.
6   Can I give *you* any help?

'I need to get to the bank this lunch hour, could you stop over and mind the phone while you have your sandwiches?'

'It's not really convenient.'

'You are the only other person who knows about the Element deal and they may be ringing.'

'Well, I usually visit Pat on Thursdays.'

'I can easily tell him on the way out. It's no trouble.'

'Thanks.'

'Look John, I have this problem with the flanges, and it seems to be in your area. I wonder if you as the expert could give me some advice . . . I have all the drawings here.' And finally, 'if there is anything you want, you know where to ask.'

The skill of the 'task manipulator' lies in developing the progression so that what is his or her problem becomes *your* problem in a smooth transition. John, in our example, began the second conversation as a free man, able to move between his states of mind as free as a bird. The 'task manipulator' is not happy with that and approaches the situation in Little Professor – 'I have this problem . . . in your area . . . I have all the drawings here.' The switch or what 'con' men call the sting, is in the last line – 'If there is anything you want, you know where to ask.' John has become the servant, the Adapted Child and the manipulator is happily able to move back to Parent and Adult, his Little Professor having done all the work. Things may well get done by this hybrid Push-Me-Pull-You problem-solver but the manipulator is quite clear who is in charge. How was it done?

In both our examples the manipulator assumes that we are in their world to help them and in our jargon of the previous chapter – the mind music that they are encouraging is concerned with our Please Me sub-theme.

The Victim will be thinking:

'Look, they're not really asking a lot.'

'They might be angry if I say no.'

'I could really.'

'I *ought* to help . . .'

We all know what the victim *ought* to say:

'I need to get to the bank this lunch hour, could you stop over and mind the phone while you have your sandwiches?'

'It's not really convenient.'

'You are the only other person who knows about the Element deal and they may be ringing.'

'It's not really convenient.'

'It's not *convenient*? Look I only asked you because I was desperate.'

'It is not convenient . . .'

But much more likely with a skilled manipulator we will either get a question:

'Are you doing something special today?'

which we feel, out of politeness that we have to answer or they could say:

'You are not usually as unhelpful as this . . .'

which is designed to make us feel guilty and apologise. Once the mind music in our heads has moved us into saying or feeling 'Sorry', we are done for.

Dealing with Criticism

The simplest and most effective way of wrong-footing anyone is to offer criticism.

'I've called you in to discuss your work . . .'

'I don't like to criticise but . . .'

'That was not a good bit of work . . .'

Criticism of any kind, justified or not, is the one way we can

almost guarantee to get anyone wrong-footed, into Adapted
Child and listening to mind music – the messages that are
remembered from our reaction to being 'told off' as little people.
As 'little people' criticism meant correction 'for doing something
wrong' against the half-understood standards of the big people's
world and we were expected to say 'Sorry', without analysis:

'You were late this morning, Smith.'

'Sorry Miss' was the automatic response then, and it still can
be now, however strong are our reasons for being late, not
completing this work, missing the post . . . We are still doing it
– saying 'Sorry' that is, as a 'knee-jerk' to adverse comment. The
'knee-jerk' reaction into an Adapted Child state of mind caused
by criticism can bring real difficulties to the 'big person' in a real
world, both as the receiver and the giver of criticism. As the
strong manager who wishes to appraise his or her staff, how do
we give positive and actionable criticism if they go on the
defensive at the slightest whiff of criticism? The difficulty for *us*
is that if we are perceived in the Parent state of mind, whatever
our intentions, our subordinates will move into Adapted Child,
and at least think 'Sorry' in their minds. The mind music of
thinking 'Sorry' incapacitates the ability to listen and respond in
Adult – there will be no dialogue.

> We were told of one manager who worked for a manager who
> certainly was perceived as invariably working from Critical Parent,
> and suffered accordingly in his relations and communications with
> his staff. The Critical Parent manager was sent by the company on
> an Interpersonal Skills course and decided to test his understanding
> immediately on returning to base. He rang his subordinate's
> secretary direct to tell her that she had been promoted.
>
> The time of the incident was in the middle of the 'Good News
> and Bad News' catch phrase from the Rowan and Martin Laugh In.
>
> 'Hallo Mary, I have two things to tell you, do you want the good
> news or the bad news first?'
>
> Mary, who was completely taken aback by the approach from a
> man it was rumoured would not know a joke if he fell over it,
> replied:
>
> 'The bad news, please.'
>
> 'Well there was a spelling mistake on the second page of the last
> memo you sent to me. But don't worry, the good news is that at
> the last board meeting it was decided that you merited a jump in
> grades. Well done Mary.'
>
> Mary was in tears when her direct manager found her. She had

heard the bad news and simply stopped listening. She had formed the impression that she was going to be fired.

The communications path Parent to Adapted Child is a one-way process and we may find that the most unlikely people can imply criticism to develop the 'Sorry' theme so that the mind music becomes deafening. For me, your author, the 'unlikely' group includes small children, ticket inspectors, my accountant . . . while I am thinking 'Sorry', I am not listening – the mind music has taken all my available energy.

So our question is:

How do you give and receive criticism constructively?

'If you don't know where you are going you will probably finish up somewhere else.'

Henry was a very mild man who liked to think about things before acting. He loved talking and often said that he was not clear what he thought about anything until he had actually said it. He was very clear about one thing – he had left his previous employer when he discovered that they were taking on a contract to supply parts for missiles. As a manager he saw himself as someone who helped to provide a 'good working environment' for his people and he was very keen to help individuals – in the language of the previous chapter, his mind music demanded that he please other people, and the overall problem was that he had been made a production manager. In our experience a certain toughness and an ability to limit the 'social worker' aspects of the job are necessary skills for production managers to remain employed, perhaps more so than with many other management roles. The production manager is normally judged by the amount of product out of the door against cost and time constraints and a soft heart is not always an advantage. The production manager is an extreme case of being judged on the consequences of his or her activity – profit, customer satisfaction . . . whereas the valued skills of the job are often concerned with the nuts and bolts of how things are done.

The situation occurred that a process worker had been repeatedly late for his shift and Henry had been forced to call him into his office for a formal verbal warning, all other procedures having been tried and failed. Immediately before the meeting in Henry's office he had been tipped off by another manager that the process worker was a keen football fan, the home team had had a replay on the

afternoon of the last lateness incident and the man had been seen
at the turnstiles.

Henry: I have to tell you that this is a disciplinary interview
          and that you have the right to have your union
          representative present.

Worker: No, that's OK. What's the trouble?

Henry: I suspect you know the trouble. You have been
          repeatedly late and last Tuesday afternoon you came
          in at the end of the shift.

Worker: Oh . . . [silence]

Henry was doing well up to now but he went on:

Henry: I don't have any real hard evidence but we think you
          went to a football match.

We do not know what Henry was hoping for, perhaps a denial
or a humble 'Sorry' but what he got was:

Worker: You are absolutely right. I was at the match – I never
          miss a match if I can help it. I'm really sorry to have
          to put you to all this trouble Mr Hamid.

Henry Hamid with his own personal mind music had a great
problem at this point. His Mind Music was full of issues about
forgiveness and 'as long as he's sorry'. It said nothing about his
position as a manager who had to uphold the position of his
foremen. It also said nothing about going back to the records
and pointing out the several other occasions that the worker
had abused the system or even that the admission of guilt
simply saved time in the process of punishing an industrial
misdemeanour.

What he *should* have done was to go back to his objectives and
find a Broken Record to play while he rallied himself. Broken
Record combined with Fielding works well and could have
sounded like this:

Henry: That's not the issue. You've been repeatedly late
          over the past five months and I have to tell you that
          you are receiving a formal verbal warning. If the
          lateness continues I have no choice but to follow the
          company procedures. (Broken Record)

Worker: I have only been a bit late and it was a home match.
          I went all the way to Goggleton for the first leg.

Henry: That again is not the point at issue. You have been
           repeatedly . . . (Fielding and Broken Record)

What Henry said in the actual situation was:

Henry: Look it really won't do. You know that even if you
           had to go to the match you should have told your
           supervisor.

Worker: You're absolutely right – I should have spoken to
           the supervisor. But he's so busy these days that I
           don't like to disturb him.

Henry allowed himself to listen to his own mind music in spite
of the fact that he would readily have acknowledged that he was
inclined to be 'a bit of a soft touch'. He also lost his way and the
process worker was beginning to exploit his weakness – 'He is so
busy these days that I don't like to disturb him' is the sort of
remark that could have enlarged the scope of the interview out
of all recognition – a clear danger sign. Henry was no longer in
control and the process worker was beginning to set up an
agenda more to his own liking. A rabbit hole has emerged in front
of Henry and he only has to say:

> 'Well the whole factory is busy and I am
> sure Mr Weston is doing his best . . .'

and anything could happen. He would be in the Catastrophe
Spiral – Henry would be defending another manager and the
process worker could very easily be able to slip into Critical
Parent. Henry has lost control of the meeting.

Basic Rules of Effective Behaviour

1 Know your own 'weaknesses' and make it as easy for
   yourself as possible.
2 If at all possible *buy time* so that you have time to plan. Be
   prepared to used Broken Record and Fielding to buy
   yourself this time.
3 Plan ahead – what needs to be done *before* any confron-
                   tation?
                 – what is your actual objective at the meeting?
                   Not what you would like to get but what you
                   have to get . . .
                 – what would you like to get from the meeting

provided you have your actual first objective?
– what do you need to do *after* the meeting?

→

EXERCISE

Think of the situation Henry found himself in.

1   Henry knew he had the particular weakness or stressor of wanting to please people. How could he have made it easier for himself?

2   What work should Henry have done before the meeting?

3   What was Henry's prime objective – what did he *have* to get out of the meeting? What should he have been prepared to do if he was not going to get it?

4   What might Henry as a professional have wanted to get out of the meeting – *provided that his prime objective had been met?*

5   What did Henry need to be able to do *AFTER* the meeting?

→

Henry wanted to be liked, but you, the reader, may well find that the 'weaknesses or stressors' that disempower you are quite different. Speaking personally, your author finds himself working less well when he is being watched by large numbers of people. About twelve people is my limit and when I am forced, as I am sometimes, to take a podium in front of hundreds, I find my knees failing. It is as if the hundreds of eyes are draining the power out of me. Some people are stressed by noise and others by silence, neither of which worries me greatly, but I do have sympathy with people who are put under pressure by time constraints, real or conjured up by a manipulator.

The situation was an industrial negotiation and the manager was handling a very difficult labour representative extremely well. The union man was very interested in the way our manager seemed to be looking at a large clock on the wall facing him and decided to try a hunch. The union man slowed down his speech and took off his own wrist watch and put it down in front of the manager. The manager's speech pattern increased pace and the union man began a very slow review of the timing of the possible labour dispute:

'Of course the present shift will be working till . . .', glance at watch, 'and that gives us about . . . let me see . . .', picks up watch and glances behind him to the clock on the wall, 'about ten minutes to sort something out . . .'

The ten minute time-limit was a fiction but the manager caved in before there was time to test it.

Many people and in particular those with Hurry Up sub-themes to their mind music find themselves panicked by the sight of others looking at their watches, and worse still by the pip-pip alarms that used to be fashionable from the then new-fangled digital watches.

Henry's problem in his interview with the football fan was not a problem with time, or with people watching or with strong emotion: it was that he wanted to please other people. On many occasions the wish to be liked and to be helpful is strictly commendable but it is hardly compatible with giving people formal verbal warnings 'leading to dismissal if the behaviour is repeated'. Henry wanted to be the nice guy and be liked by everyone; therefore a disciplinary situation would be predictably hard for him. He probably worried in advance but worry is not enough – we need to act.

We would see that understanding the situations that give you personal stress is half the battle – your author knows he is stressed by 'eyes watching him' so even with a minor complaint to a shop with returned goods, will choose a quiet day and ask to see the manager out of the main shop-area. People stressed by time may choose to stay over in the hotel on the previous night to a conference to take the personal pressures off. They know that a single motorway hold-up will reduce their effectiveness on arrival and you really do not have to explain in detail your actions to other people. People without your personal stressor may well be unsympathetic but this is irrelevant.

> You are judged by your performance
> and not by your excuses.

Think ahead and if you see potential trouble – *plan*. Henry in his situation of disciplining a member of his team knew that he was doing something 'against his nature' and therefore he had to work tightly to a script and really plan – any deviation from the script could be expected to cause him problems and possibly make him act in response to his mind music.

Let's look in detail at how Henry could have planned for the meeting with the process worker. Henry needs to do quite a lot of homework before the meeting. How many times had the process worker been late before this occasion and how late had he been? Had he ever forged his attendance sheets? Had he been spoken to, and, if so, by whom? Were there any other issues that were known about the man? Henry might also need to revise his knowledge of the company's formal and informal disciplinary procedures. The Aware Manager needs to go into a difficult situation with as much information as possible, but gaps in knowledge can always occur. Suppose Henry had missed some vital point:

> Worker: I quite often let people think I'm going to a match, get seen at the turnstiles and that, but I have to visit my brother. He's in gaol and I don't like to talk about it. Your predecessor knew all about it and allowed me time off, provided I made it up, and settled it in some way with the supervisor.

If this happens it is advisable for most people, and certainly the Henrys of the world to say:

> Henry: I was unaware of that and it brings a new perspective to the issue. I will need some more time to check it out. You are on the same shift tomorrow – yes? – OK back in here at 3 tomorrow.

Henry, provided there are to be no surprises, has two related prime objectives. He is a representative of the hierarchy of management and he must make sure that the process worker respects this hierarchy by maintaining control in the meeting. If he has a history of 'being a soft touch' – Henry's own words – the maintenance of control will be all the more difficult, and if he fails to maintain control, then he must terminate the meeting. Once he has established 'who's in charge' he needs to provide the legal foundation for the company's disciplinary procedure. He needs to establish a formal verbal warning. If he finds himself unable to do that then the interview with the employee is not the correct place for argument. His 'hoped for' objective, once he has given the formal warning might be to develop some procedure for the man to be on time. If Henry allows problem-solving to mix with the disciplinary aspects, then he is very likely to be manipulated.

Even during the planning before the meeting, Henry needs to concern himself with what may be necessary to do later. He needs to check on the system for the formal recording of the interview – what exactly is the company procedure for this? He will probably need to inform other persons in the organisation – who and how? He may also expect to look into the organisation of the worker's section and the follow-up – how could this be done?

Henry also needs to think about the logistics of the meeting – is it to be in his office and should anyone else be present? Should he remain seated or stand by the window? Obviously he must avoid accidental disturbance but should he arrange for 'help to be at hand'? Can he fix the time so that he will be able to relax for a few minutes before the meeting?

Success in a potentially stressful situation is a lot easier after you have planned thoroughly and you can devote all of your energy to the single problem on hand. It is virtually impossible to have foreseen every twist but the very process of thinking about things in advance makes it easier to cope with the un-expected. It is not always possible to plan and do things in the ideal way for you, but it is much more often possible than most of us think.

George Washington and the apple tree – 'I cannot tell a lie, it was me'

We have discussed the interview from Henry's standpoint but we have not looked at it from the process worker's position. *How* did the process worker deal with the criticism in such a devastating way? Let's look at the words the worker used:

'You are absolutely right, I was at the match . . .'

The process worker simply accepted the criticism and killed the topic dead, what else was there for Henry to say about it. There was no 'sorry' implied in any form. The worker did not Blame, Justify, Explain . . . any of those things in Adapted Child that would have allowed Henry to go into Critical Parent:

'Well it was only one afternoon and it was an important match.'

– still accepting that he was at the match but inviting the reply from Henry:

'Whether it was an important match or not is not the point. You were absent without leave and . . .'

– Henry stays in control.

Henry was hoping, if not exactly demanding, that the process worker would take on an Adapted Child state of mind and he did not get it. The worker stayed in Adult (possibly Little Professor) and used APPROPRIATE ASSERTION: he admitted the truth in a firm and positive way so that all future discussion of the matter was irrelevant. Appropriate Assertion can be a devastating reply to any form of criticism – true or untrue – and makes sure that you do not reward the person criticising you by going into an Adapted Child state of mind and feeling 'sorry'. It can of course be a dangerous tactic to adopt if you find yourself using it frequently.

APPROPRIATE ASSERTION

For valid or invalid criticism from an aggressor
who demands you as an Adapted Child
accept or reject appropriately and mean it

Use a firm level tone and catch the other's eyes

Kill the topic dead – do not allow further discussion

Use some of the other's words if possible

If you find that you are beginning to trust the other person

move on to a constructive enquiry of what is meant.

EXERCISE

Make two lists on a note pad:

List A.   Totally invalid comments and criticism of you

List B.   Valid criticisms.

If possible get a colleague to do the same and swap lists and read the lists to each other.

Use these forms of words as appropriate:

'That is completely untrue, I am not . . .', his or her words.
or
'You are absolutely correct, I am . . .', his or her words.

If you have no human mirror to work on, use a bathroom mirror and watch your own eyes. Did you really mean it? If you did and 'they' believe you, try to learn something from the criticism – why do you say that? What exactly is the issue? Be very careful and if you have any doubts about the potential of the personal criticism as a source of help, forget it.

⟶

The combination of Appropriate Assertion, Broken Record and Fielding can be formidable, but we have mentioned 'moving on to a constructive enquiry', and CONSTRUCTIVE ENQUIRY will be the last of the techniques we are going to discuss. The premise for using Constructive Enquiry is that criticism is seldom, however well-intentioned, in the form that is useful to us.

'I've called you in to discuss your work . . .'

'I don't like to criticise but . . .'

'That was not a good bit of work . . .'

'I've called you in to discuss your work' is likely to be followed by:

'and it's not good enough – pull your socks up!'

None of those comments is a lot of help. What we need to know is that particular bits of our work *can* and *need* to be improved. The global aspects of the 'pull your socks up' advice are useless.

'What particular aspects of my work are giving you concern?'

brings the general into the specific and allows us to learn. Criticism properly handled is our window to the world – it is the 'giftie gie us, to see oursels as others see us!' Constructive

Enquiry is the movement forward from criticism in the same way as Workable Compromise was the movement forward from the buying time of Broken Record and Fielding.

Making the most of valued criticism

CONSTRUCTIVE ENQUIRY

If you are sure that the other is NOT attempting to manipulate you –

SET UP A DIALOGUE AND LEARN

Admit the element of truth in the criticism

ask for clarification – how it affects them

– what you could do?

Be gentle – Constructive Enquiry can devastate your allies

The issue of being gentle when using Constructive Enquiry is very important. On the whole, few people are used to dealing with people who actually want to communicate. Much of our conversation outside work itself is designed to be nothing more than social chit-chat establishing a basic contact and perhaps proclaiming a relationship. What we take as a criticism and may decide to develop, could have been a casual remark from someone else and the last thing they expect is for us to attempt to develop it into a meaningful dialogue.

EXERCISE

Complete the following dialogue using BROKEN RECORD, FIELDING, WORKABLE COMPROMISE, APPROPRIATE ASSERTION and CONSTRUCTIVE ENQUIRY. The characters are Joan, Director of a market research organisation and Kathy, an Area Manager.

Boss: I have to tell you that your results for the year were unsatisfactory.

Sub.: I find that difficult to accept. My area is particularly difficult – you know that.

Boss: Use FIELDING and BROKEN RECORD

Sub.: OK, that's all very well – but consider some of the people I've been foisted with. Old Green let the whole thing slip and now you're blaming me.

Boss: Use FIELDING and BROKEN RECORD

Sub.: That's still completely unfair.

Boss: Use FIELDING and BROKEN RECORD

Sub.: What you are doing is setting me up. If I got reasonable instructions, I might be able to function effectively.

Boss: Use APPROPRIATE ASSERTION

Sub.: Rubbish! You don't care a damn. Everyone knows that.

Boss: Use APPROPRIATE ASSERTION

Sub.: You're right, perhaps I was a little strong. However, your instructions are pretty awful. I have no idea of what you want. Today's interview came as a complete surprise.

Boss: Use APPROPRIATE ASSERTION followed by CONSTRUCTIVE ENQUIRY

Sub.: Well, am I in the new client business, or is expanding the existing business what you want? I have no idea.

Boss: I see it as a bit of both.

Sub.: I need more than that.

Boss: Move to WORKABLE COMPROMISE

⟶

A possible script is over the page but before you turn over – think of what might have happened if Joan, the boss, had listened to her mind music. What sort of messages could have been going round her head when Kathy said – 'You don't care a damn', and what could she have replied?

One possible completed script using the techniques could be:

Boss: I have to tell you that your results for the year were unsatisfactory.

Sub.: I find that difficult to accept. My area is particularly difficult – you know that.

Boss: I agree that there are problems in your area but even allowing for those, your year was unsatisfactory.

Sub.: OK, that's all very well, but consider some of the people I've had foisted onto me. Old Green let the whole thing slip and now you're blaming me.

Boss: I may sound as if I'm blaming you unfairly but I still have to tell you that your year was not as expected in this organisation.

Sub.: That's still completely unfair.

Boss: Perhaps, but everything considered we still come to the fact that your performance for the year was not up to standard.

Sub.: What you are doing is setting me up. If I got reasonable instructions, I might be able to function effectively.

Boss: I assure you that I am not setting you up. It is simply your last year's figures that we are discussing. They reflected badly on all of us.

Sub.: Rubbish! You don't care a damn. Everyone knows that.

Boss: That is completely untrue. I am vitally concerned with all members of my staff, as managers and people.

Sub.: Sorry, perhaps I was a little strong. However, your instructions are pretty awful. I never have any idea what you want. Today's interview came as a complete surprise.

Boss: I accept that that is a valid criticism of the way we are communicating. How would you think we could get our corporate objectives over to you as an area manager?

Sub.: Well, am I in the new client business or is expanding the existing business what you want? I have no idea.

Boss: I see it as a bit of both.

Sub.:   I need more than that.

Boss: Obviously this needs more work. If I arranged a meet-
        ing for all the area managers on the topic of setting
        Objectives, Standards and Targets, would that help?

Sub.:   I think it would.

The Aware Manager not only needs to be able to receive criticism
effectively, he or she also needs to be able to give others
actionable comments – constructive help. The rules for giving
constructive help are derived from our techniques of Appropriate
Assertion and Constructive Enquiry.

GUIDELINES FOR CONSTRUCTIVE FEEDBACK

Practicalities

Focus on the positive and be seen to be constructive

Be clear and explain why *you* are giving the feedback

Talk about specifics and things that can be changed

Choose the time and place with care – avoid public scenes

Plan what you intend to say and close with a summary

Remember you have two ears and one mouth – a good
counsellor focuses and catalyses but does not originate

Techniques

Start on common ground – be clear and take responsibility

Watch your own and the other person's body language

Meter your own effectiveness

Make the ground rules clear –
explain what is confidential and what is not

Show respect, listen and never ever persecute

You Sit There where I Can See You

There is another form of manipulation which is not really about
doing things but about insisting that those around us adopt a

stereotyped role suitable to us, whether the stereotype is appropriate or not for the task in hand. For example I am certain the reader will recognise some people in our working lives who always seem to structure our time with them so that we are in a subservient role, regardless of the circumstances. If we attempt to move from the subservient role they have chosen for us, somehow we find ourselves being 'put down'. These people have preferred Critical Parent and Adult states of mind and to stay in those states *we have to be manoeuvred into Adapted Child*. With their Critical Parent and Adult and our Child state, we have a symbiosis that is comfortable for them and they work to get such a symbiosis. These people we will call 'role manipulators'.

A role manipulator has preferred states of mind
To achieve these states the role manipulator needs others to be in complementary states, whether they agree or not and whether these roles are appropriate to the circumstances or not.

If the 'role manipulator' likes to be in charge, to give orders and organise or to protect, he or she needs somebody to give orders to, to be organised or to be protected. If, on the other hand, the role manipulator prefers to be in Adapted Child, he or she will always look for someone to rescue or to persecute him or her – a Nurturing Parent or a Critical Parent. In what seems to be an entirely unconscious way they structure their lives to be in their preferred states of mind. Unfortunately, they often attempt to structure our lives in the process.

I visited an old people's rehabilitation hospital recently with a well-meaning amateur but hospital visitor. One of the old people was refusing her dinner and the well-meaning visitor moved immediately to the old lady and began to coax her to eat with a spoon:

'Come on, you have to eat something. It's very nice.'

The Sister of the ward took the visitor gently aside and said:

'I'd be grateful if you didn't do that: our job here is to get the old people back to doing things for themselves.'

The visitor liked helping people and using a well-developed Nurturing Parent. Like the Boy Scout with the knife forever hoping to find a horse with a stone in its hoof, the visitor was always looking for an opportunity to use her very special skill. She would have liked to cast the old lady in an Adapted Child role – a role that

the Sister found inappropriate. The amateur hospital visitor preferred to be in Nurturing Parent and *required* an Adapted Child in
order to be happy.

With the 'role manipulator' it is almost as if they need your Child,
or your Parent so that they can function as a whole person and
if you are assertive and refuse to be role-cast, they move over to
someone else less particular and you lose their acquaintance. The
'role manipulator' demands that you enter into his or her game
and relinquish any right to autonomy. You may feel the role they
have chosen for you is a role you are comfortable playing but this
is not always so. There must be a choice, and the choice must be
yours.

It is very important that we expand the issue of choice. When
we join say the Army, we accept that on the whole, we will
remain in an Adapted Child state of mind to our superior officers
and, if we have a rank ourselves, that those below us will accept
our Parent and Adult to their Child. The manager often finds him
or herself in Parent and Adult and their staff in Adapted Child –
it makes for one sort of working entity – a symbiosis. This is a
consciously accepted and possibly negotiated contract, but the
role manipulator makes no such negotiation – you *will* be in
Parent or *you* will be in Adapted Child.

The world is organised so that for many jobs the symbiosis is
negotiable on completing the application form for the job – we
are introduced to the boss and our subordinates and for many
purposes the rules are set:

'I do the thinking on this job; you just do it.'

I have heard this on interview, and at least with this approach
you know the score. This type of authoritarian boss uses his or
her Parent/Adult states of mind for the management style and
recruits Adapted Children to do the work. The understood and
acceptable symbiosis is fine, but the 'role manipulator' may well
extend the boundary of the relationship, and demand fixed states
of mind from others not just for the task in hand but from the
human being underneath.

Forcing other people into a set role and pattern of behaviour
can have very serious consequences both for the role manipulator
and the 'victim'.

Lionel is a senior police officer who presents a private and public
face of professional concern for his job. About five years ago he
arrived at an incident in a rather weather-beaten area in the inner

city for which he has responsibility. The homes had seen better days
and were inevitably moving from family homes to squats and the
bulldozer. One particular house, the scene of aimless vandalism
was still owned and occupied by two middle-aged spinster sisters.
Lionel charmed the sisters and assisted them personally through
the rather distasteful process of identification parades and court-
rooms. From then on he received small tributes in the form of cakes
and home-made jams from the ladies. They began to appear in his
office and finally outside his home on a range of pretexts. At first
he was happy to help drafting a letter to the Council opposing a
compulsory purchase order, but it went on. He began to dread
going to work and used his wife to check whether the ladies were
going to ambush him on his way to the office.

Finally he was forced to take out a restraining order on the ladies.

What had happened to Lionel? The two ladies, by skill or accident
had acted as 'role manipulators' and had forced him to continue
a symbiotic relationship where they were both in Adapted Child
and he was in Adult/Nurturing Parent. Originally the relationship was appropriate – they did need professional help – but the
continuation was not. It had happened in good faith, probably
from all three human beings, but it produced an intolerable
situation for Lionel and ended in very bad feelings for everyone.

Many people find themselves being used in some form of
symbiosis by others and ultimately what can become a form of
slavery makes them have to take drastic action. The solution is
'not to start from here'. By using the techniques described in the
two last chapters you will be able to review the mind music that
makes you prey to the accidental or deliberate 'task' and 'role
manipulator'. It may be perfectly OK for you to provide caring
support for one member of staff and act as a pair of hands for
another, but be aware of what you are doing. A symbiosis is
easier to drift into than escape from.

→

EXERCISE

Review the relationships you have in work with subordinates,
peers and bosses and see whether any of them are locked into
what we have termed symbiosis. It is probable for instance,
that the Parent to Child balance progresses down the hierarchy
but is it inviolate? To be effective it is necessary at times to be
Adapted Child and *listen* to your subordinates and to be Critical

Parent and *tell* your boss. Realistically, is this possible for you? If it is not possible, what would you see as the personal adverse consequences?

———————➤

Before we progress out of the area of assertive behaviour we feel that we ought to issue a 'Government Health Warning'. Ordinary people are inclined to value you for the role they perceive you in. The 'nice guy' has a place, as does the mild bully. We have shown you how to break the mould and in breaking the mould you may well lose the casual friendship of others. You may also be seen as a threat to others at work.

This chapter ends the first part of the book. In the second part of the book we will be looking much more at the actual management job and employing skills. We will start with 'the meeting' and how this can be made more effective by the use of commonsense methods. We will then show that some of the problems of the meeting arise because we use our 'valued skills' inappropriately. A discipline of using techniques can get over this issue but a very simple classification of 'valued skills' allows us to understand how best to motivate, instruct and supervise others, including your boss.

CHAPTER FIVE

The Meeting:
Working with Individuals
and Groups – Where the
Differences Matter

'I go to a meeting thinking it's for one thing and it turns out to be for something completely different.'

'When I think I am being asked to help with a decision and then find out that it is all cut and dried, I feel really bad.'

'Often I find I'm only asked to attend so that I can share the blame if it fails.'

'We start to tackle a problem sensibly and soon they are all over the place – dashing hither and thither and nobody listening to anyone else.'

'When we finish a meeting I go back to my office, relax for a moment and start on the minutes as if the meeting never happened.'

The book is about the change focus. Up to now we have concentrated on the Aware Manager and his or her one-to-one relations. Now we are going to move ahead and use the information we have gathered about each other for the more obvious tasks of management – controlling people in teams and groups. We will begin with that dreaded beast – the formal meeting.

Although many of us seem to spend more of our productive time at meetings than doing anything else, most of us will find the basic point in the John Cleese film *Meetings Bloody Meetings* far from funny. In the film a manager explains to his wife that he has to do *all* his work at home because he spends his entire official working day at unproductive meetings. The film then goes on to explain how meetings can be made effective and that the responsibility for this lies with the managers concerned. We agree. The techniques for making both formal and informal meetings productive are sensible and quite easily learned but in practice we have found the techniques difficult to 'enforce'.

In this chapter we will look at the objectives of meetings and talk very briefly about using two techniques for improving their efficiency. We will then relate some of the common problems in meetings to our idea of 'valued skills'. In our discussion we will find that we can begin to look at the differences between individuals in terms of the way they tackle problems and see how specific 'medicines' can be applied to the problem-solving processes of organisations and groups. Our view is that the basic management job is one of problem-solving and on that basis we will use our concepts of individual differences to discuss communication, recruitment and the issues of briefing subordinates, peers and even one's bosses. The expansion of the concepts towards management communications will form the subject of the next chapter, but before this we need to discuss the vexed subject of meetings.

The Basic Issue of the Confused Meeting

A very senior British civil servant who as part of his job writes the minutes for Cabinet meetings is quoted as explaining his strategy for the job as:

> 'I certainly never write what they say or even what they should have said. I write down what they would have liked to have said if they had had the time to consider things properly.'

→

EXERCISE

Look at your last working week and consider how much of it was concerned with formal meetings.

Divide the time into:

Preparation – Travelling – The actual meeting – Post work

Look at each meeting you attended and consider what was the

purpose of the meeting and what was your purpose in attending it.

Think about the time *after* the meeting. Did you find yourself motivated to further work or did you 'take time to recover'?

⟶

Meetings can cost horrendous amounts of money and can take up a great deal of our *active* time. The money aspect can be calculated and I know of one organisation who used to present a colour slide at the beginning of each meeting. The slide showed pallets of the company products to the approximate value of the time expected to be devoted to the meeting. As with many other good ideas, the joke soon wore thin and the practice of showing the slide was stopped, but not before the number of meetings and their duration had been severely reduced. The slide related to direct costs – the demotivational effect of the wasted or tedious meeting is less easy to assess. How much does it cost *later* in productive time to be frustrated or bored out of our minds:

'I go to a meeting thinking it's for one thing and it turns out to be for something completely different.'

'Often I feel I'm only asked to attend so that I can share the blame if it fails.'

I would see the formal meeting as having four distinct possible purposes:

CONTROL

COMMUNICATION

DECISION-MAKING

PROBLEM-SOLVING

The meeting designed to demonstrate **control** is perfectly legitimate and more common than we might first like to admit. The whole ritualistic mechanism of the formal meeting – agenda, a chairperson with particular privileges, standing orders, minutes, time constraints, formality of seating . . . can all be used as mechanisms to demonstrate 'who's in charge' and formalise the

'role manipulation' – that is, if managers wish to play it that way.
The control procedures of meetings can also be modified to signal
that an Adult manager is taking over.

> The formality of some German companies is still a surprise to many
> foreigners and in the company we were working with it was taken
> to excess at meetings where the previous Chief Executive attended.
> The new man watched how the meetings worked and decided to
> make changes.
>
> What used to happen was that all the managers, other than the
> Chief Executive would arrive slightly early for the meeting and
> indulge in quiet small talk. At five minutes after the prescribed
> time, the Chief Executive would come in and, with all his staff
> standing at attention, would walk round each in turn shaking hands
> and making ritual conversation. The whole process took some thirty
> minutes and only after it was completed could they all sit down and
> begin the meeting. The meeting itself was run in a very author-
> itarian manner and any real exchange of views and opinions only
> happened after the Chief Executive had left.
>
> The new manager, coming from another German company
> operating in Sri Lanka had different ideas. He was waiting for his
> managers as they came in, started the meeting on time with no
> ceremony and expected real participation from his staff. Several of
> them preferred the old ways and began looking for jobs elsewhere.

The meeting can also be a fine way of allowing information to be
shared between relevant colleagues. The formal meeting allows
information to be presented *simultaneously* and permits *feedback*,
albeit under a measure of control. Since it allows feedback it also
allows a change of tactics by management if the information or
the method of presentation needs to be revised in the light of its
reception by the meeting. The written document does not allow
such a revision.

The discipline of the meeting permits a chosen group to tackle
problems. Because all the group can be involved with the preparation of potential solutions, there is a high chance that all the
group will be committed to the implementation of these solutions. The formal meeting does help problem-solving in that the
features of control and formality allow structured approaches.
The 'sit down and listen' side of the formal meeting can well help
the communication of complex ideas from experts to those
involved with execution of those ideas. Not only do we have to
'sit down and listen' but also we are seen by others to have been

allowed to understand. The joke that a camel was a horse designed by a committee has been attacked from many sides, including the cynics who considered it as being unfair to camels. It is certainly unfair to the well-conducted meeting where everyone present 'knows where they are' by the closure. The worst type of meeting occurs when those present feel they are being used to fudge a decision or share the blame of the inevitable.

> The good chairperson is able to develop consensus views or at least understand where these are not possible.

→

EXERCISE

Think of examples of a meeting you have attended recently where:

Control
Communication
Decision-making
Problem-solving

predominated.

Were you aware before the meeting of its main purpose and why you were present?

If you were not aware, would it have helped if you had been told and how could you have been told?

How would you judge the 'efficiency' of any meeting?

Rate your meetings on your criteria and suggest what could have been done to improve the ratings.

→

The formal meeting provides the **control** that assists the purposes of communication, decision-making and problem-solving but certain meetings are designed to demonstrate control alone. I can think of at least two examples where the senior management used tricks of stage management to ensure that clear and effective control was demonstrated in the chosen theatre of the formal meeting.

YES, BUT LET'S HEAR WHAT MR BROWN HAS TO SAY

The Executive Manager of an R&D department had a very authoritarian style in an organisation full of intelligent but diverse voices. He worked through small informal 'advisory' meetings with individual members of staff (we shall later term this an A11 style of management) but his 'formal' meetings nearly always included all the relevant staff and were massive. His 'cabinet' of section heads and divisional managers numbered about thirty and he was fully aware that a meeting of such a size could not work for purposes other than demonstrating control.

On this and all other occasions the agenda was formal and blocked with pre-published reports but certain items were presented 'for discussion'. This time the discussion was not showing a consensus for the advice that the Executive wanted and there was beginning to be some agreement against his views from his usually divided managers. He turned round to a silent member of the group and accused the assembly of not listening to every shade of opinion.

The previously silent member presented a divergent opinion and the Chief Executive demanded that it be recorded in the minutes that there was 'a division of opinion on the matter'.

He then took this prompted division of opinion as licence to act as he had previously thought fit.

LET'S HEAR IT FOR . . .

The Chief Executive of another company would detail his annual plans with the full paraphernalia of audio-visual aids, including the latest in computer graphics. He would present his division managers rather as a chat show host. Put on the rostrum with applause and another peer waiting in the wings, it was a virtually impossible situation for any of the divisional managers to move from the tight brief imposed upon him or her. No dissenting voices were ever heard in public.

To some extent all of us can employ the tricks of authority on those around us. We may allocate particular tasks to particular members of staff so that their contribution is reduced – there are always 'cabinet' posts which like real Cabinet posts, are on the face of it promotions but in fact act as a poisoned chalice. The skilled manager may shy off the too obvious tactic of writing his or her own minutes *and* setting the agenda but we will probably have had one trick of control played on us. We will have been inveigled into accepting the task of taking the minutes for someone else's meeting only to find that the chairperson has reserved the right to vet and change the minutes after we have completed the job to our satisfaction.

More subtle is the manager who uses seating arrangements to squash, amplify or neutralise conflict and maintain control. The use of sunlight to avoid eye contact may be a little obvious but giving the dissenting voice the 'right hand' position of seating position is very effective indeed – it is possible to cut out anyone sitting on your right-hand side by the most imperceptible of body movements. Similarly people with opposing views can be made to face each other across a table to augment conflict or side by side to attempt reconciliation. The skilled Little Professor manager acting as chairperson can make manipulative moves scarcely without anyone knowing what has happened. The chairperson is in a position to enforce control in a meeting by a variety of tactics – for clear, firm decision by blocking the possibility of group involvement or to relax control so as to make co-operative problem-solving possible.

---->

EXERCISE

Think of a particular formal meeting you have attended recently.

Looking back, did the structure of the room, the seating arrangements, 'dramatis personae', give you direct clues as to the purpose of the meeting and your expected role?

Think of some of the situations you found difficult from the last chapter and how by what we have called 'stage management' you could have both reduced your own stressors and maintained control of the situation.

---->

A junior civil servant was discussing his inability to influence the course of formal meetings he attended. The meetings were conducted in a long room with a bespoke long table and formal seating plan. The senior person at the meeting was in the centre of one long face and our junior was on the same side on the far left. In this position he could never catch the chairperson's eye without resorting to bizarre behaviour, and we felt that such a situation had not happened by chance. The junior was at the meeting as a recording witness and not as a participant and to keep his job he better believe it.

In any organisation we can **communicate** by a range of methods:

1   By meeting people on an individual basis – one-to-one
2   In informal meetings
3   In formal meetings
4   By phone or electronic 'mail'
5   In writing to a restricted and directed circulation
6   In writing to the mass.

The choice of medium for conveying the communication obviously depends on the message, the sender and the recipient. Some messages need the privacy of a one-to-one, while others are best stuck on the noticeboard for all to see. The formal or chaired medium is only one way of communicating and has to make its claim over the other media – writing a memo could be simpler and on the face of it – cheaper. What has the formal meeting got to commend it?

The Case for the Formal Meeting

The chosen audience get, as far as is humanly possible, the same message at the same time.

Feedback and clarification is possible and in fact likely.

The actual message can be restricted in circulation and put in a relevant context.

Partial and unconsidered information can be included.

The message can be modified in the light of reactions.

Obviously there are disadvantages as well as advantages in these characteristics, but most of these disadvantages can be got over using the formal meeting in conjunction with the other media – notes to the agenda or a reinforcing handout at the close. We may choose to meet certain of the participants on a one-to-one basis before or after the meeting and we may choose to issue minutes. The reader may well remember the quotation at the beginning of the chapter about the minutes of government meetings and be able to think of minutes as *the actionable outcome of a getting together, and not necessarily a record of the action when we got together*. Overall the formal meeting has one great advantage over any other medium – it allows the person calling the meeting to judge the temperature of the reception of the message and adjust the message accordingly for future circulation. The formal meeting can also be a formidable demonstration of control or of naked power.

An impressive example of the use of a meeting to convey power and as a form of communication occurred when a senior executive was being removed by a large organisation.

All the line managers were instructed to attend a meeting at 11.00 in a large conference room by a note carried round by messenger when they had just arrived in their offices.

The senior executive came in one end of the conference room at 11.01 and made the following speech:

'As from 11.00 today I have handed over responsibility for this division to Dr Bloggo. This statement is being posted on all staff noticeboards at this moment.

'I would like to introduce you to Dr Bloggo, who is standing at the other end of the room. I hope that you will give him the same devoted support you have given to me in the past. Goodbye and thank you.'

Dr Bloggo thanked the retiring incumbent, confirmed his statement and closed the meeting. The whole operation took three minutes.

→

EXERCISE

Look back at the examples of meetings you remembered and in particular the meeting you saw as being designed to communicate. In the light of what we have discussed:

Was the formal meeting the most satisfactory medium of communication?

Should other media have been used in addition to the meeting?

Decision-making meetings probably give us all the greatest worry, a worry which is echoed by two statements at the beginning of this chapter:

'When I think I am being asked to help with a decision and find out that it is all cut and dried, I feel really bad.'

'Often I feel I'm only asked to attend so that I can share the blame if it fails.'

You arrive in a meeting expecting to use your Adult state of mind and suddenly find that you are being manipulated into sharing blame for a decision that has already been made – and you should have been in Adapted Compliant Child all the time. There was no seat for your Adult round the table. In Chapter 7 we will discuss how you, as a good manager, can make sure that your staff understand what is required of them, but in the meantime let's get down to a few ground rules.

If a formal or chaired meeting is genuinely being asked to make a decision, the first issue that needs to be established is the relationship of the meeting members to the outcome of the decision and its implementation. If their commitment is not required, then any process, arbitrary or logical, can be used. If each and every member needs to contribute personally and unsupervised to the implementation, then consensus must be reached. At some point between personal irrelevance and absolute commitment, the majority will can be allowed to prevail.

A group of managers controlling the operations of foreign subsidiaries in a multinational were called together to decide on a policy concerned with the acceptance of 'inducements' for the granting of favours. The overall company policy was that bribery in any form was a sacking offence, but in some of the geographical areas of the company's operation, 'dash' was endemic.

Once the decision had been made, each and every manager had to apply the policy locally and policing by the central authority was virtually impossible.

Our example is that of a decision-making meeting that required a consensus view and any form of enforcement by the chairperson or by 'democratic' vote would have been a waste of time. Any of the managers, returning to their home base and disagreeing with the decision of the meeting, was capable of damaging sabotage, and any voting procedures would simply have identified and alienated the minorities. As has been said before – 'You only call for a vote when you have a majority on your side.' If you need the minority on your side as well . . .

The guidelines for effective decision-making meetings are:

1 Everyone at the meeting must know why they are at the meeting and be give as much time to prepare as possible.

2 Each member of the meeting must be able to contribute to the level of his or her expertise and relevance.

3 The 'expert' on the decision must be able to enlighten but not to dominate.

4 The 'user' of the decision must be clearly identified and given a defined time to comment on potential solutions.

5 Techniques, such as those proposed in the next section of this chapter may be used to obtain structure to the process of the meeting but they must not be allowed to force logic over the gut feelings of the individuals present.

6 There is very, very rarely enough information available for a completely rational decision and most often logic takes you only half the way.

The bad decision-making process forgets the facts of management life and feigns logic when common sense would have seen otherwise. The Aware Manager needs to be particularly watchful of the computer-borne analysis of the expert – garbage in, garbage out.

7 **The consensus decision-making process cannot be hurried.**

> Parkinson in his brilliant book describing his Law quotes the story of the Electric Utility Company who took two hours on the siting of a car park and two minutes to decide on the form of an atomic reactor.

Time must be allocated to consensus decision-making process in relation to the importance of that particular decision. The Synectics Organisation recommends a time-structured approach to meetings. In this approach each item for discussion is allocated a set time-span in the agenda and the chairperson makes sure that this time is not exceeded. In practice I have found the very threat of such a draconian from of meeting control is enough to make a group feel that you are serious in wanting the meetings to earn their corn and the group will impose its own discipline.

8   Always allow for second thoughts in major decisions.

For any major decision there must be some form of double assembly – the Senate and the House of Representatives, the Commons and the Lords. The comments of the British Cabinet secretary at the beginning of this chapter are important – we need to act on what we would have said if we had had time to consider – the action loving meeting spends a great deal of its life repairing the damage of its own actions.

People in meetings do get excited and carried away and there *must* be time to reflect. The Aware Manager has probably already learnt *never* to post a difficult or angry letter on the day of writing but always to review it, hopefully with a third party, in the cold light of the next morning – and so it is with important decisions.

9   The decision-making meeting needs some form of record after it has been concluded.

MINUTES.   Minutes are most likely to be used for control and the control is probably from outside the meeting.

ACTION MINUTES.   The action minute, as its name implies, names responsibility, gives deal-lines and states objectives. It is brief, apolitical and *actionable* (See p. 86).

Action minutes are agreed at the meeting itself and their circulation is almost immediate.

RECORDS.   The 'record of meeting' is a political document designed for posterity and is the form of meeting referred to by the Cabinet Secretary. They are paramount in the control of an organisation, and the stir caused when a member of the meeting – a disgruntled Cabinet Minister for instance – writes his or her memoirs to repudiate the records, is real.

Records of meetings need to be written by a person of sufficient stature to understand points in their organisational context. They should be brief and of as restricted circulation as possible. They should not be confused with the Public Relations document – the Prepared Statement.

━━━━━▶

EXERCISE

Consider a recent and complex decision your organisation has

ACTION MINUTES

Reference Number:	Project Title:	
A/c Number:	Date:	
Purpose of Meeting:		
Circulation:	Venue:	
	Present:	
Summary of meeting:		
ACTIONS by whom:		Review Date:

had to make. In the light of what we have discussed:

Could the decision process have been made more effective?

Were the participants well-briefed, clear of their roles and involved with the solutions offered?

If asked, how could you recommend the reporting procedures of your organisation be improved?

$$\longrightarrow$$

The **problem-solving** meeting requires more than the possibility of feedback – it depends upon it. In my previous book, *The New Manager*, I recommended the Kepner Tregoe approach for structuring a problem-solving meeting. The Kepner Tregoe approach treats every problem in a purely logical way and conducts the proceedings in a number of distinct stages as shown on page 88.

The whole Kepner Tregoe system in my own direct experience works well in practice *but* requires a measure of control over the whole process and that very control may counter-balance the gains in rationality it produces. We are therefore recommending a simpler if perhaps less refined approach. The initial stages of problem analysis could be seen as asking *Why?* – why we need to do any work in the first place. We then ask ourselves *what?* could be done to face the issues from the agreed *Why?* questions and we seek alternatives. If we were using the unmodified Kepner Tregoe system we would move towards solving the problem – the *How?* we could do it. Finally when we have decided on the *How?* questions we take action, looking simultaneously at the consequences – the *'If?'* we do that, what will be the consequences?

$$\longrightarrow$$

EXERCISE

Read the following dialogue and label it in terms of *Why?* anything is being proposed, *What?* is being proposed, *How?* it is going to be tackled and what the consequences are likely to be – the *If?* questions.

'I feel that we need to move the offices. It's much too difficult

The Kepner Tregoe System of Problem-Solving

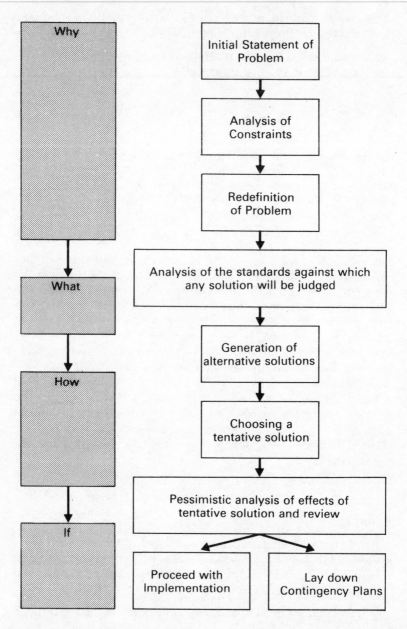

to get multilingual staff here for our Continental Europe operation.'

'What exactly are you proposing? Are you saying that we need to close the London office altogether?'

'The ground rent is too high but if we move out of London, how many people will stay with the company? How do we get skilled WP operators in Cornwall?'

'Who said anything about Cornwall? Mind you the winters are milder there.'

I think we should keep some of the operation in London and use modems. The number of people who tell me that they would like to work from home . . .'

'And it's easier for the kids – continuity of schooling . . .'

→

The style of the discussion is probably familiar to most of us but we probably still find some difficulty seeing any sensible sequence. The sensible sequence would have been to discuss *Why?* there is an issue first and once there is an agreement on the problem to continue onto *What?* could be done. Once the *What?* questions have been answered we can decide on the *How?* questions and then the *If?* consequences – otherwise we waste a lot of time. For instance suppose on reflection the *Why?* issue is only concerned with office space for clerical staff. The *What?* alternatives could well include Modems and FAX machines connected to the London office from anywhere in Europe. The *How?* questions are then honed down to technical and timing issues – the cost could be 'ball courted' to establishing telephone lines, satellite links and the like. The *If?* questions are concerned with security, computer hackers and power failures. None of these issues would have any high relevance if we have decided that the *Why?* issue was concerned with having the corporate base nearer EEC headquarters. In that case a whole new chain would have been relevant. The sequence *Why?* – *What?* – *How?* – *If?* is fundamental to successful problem-solving.

WHY	WHAT	HOW	IF
questions	questions	questions	questions
Why are we concerned?	What could solve the concerns?	How do we do what is being proposed?	If we do that what would be the result?

We then, in important issues, need to recycle back to the *Why?* questions. Does what we are proposing, given all the consequences, still meet our concerns?

Let's stay with the problem of the offices in London and look at the *Why?* questions:

We cannot get skilled linguists in London.

Office space in London is very expensive.

The Managing Director has a home in Cornwall.

The focus of the operation is moving to Brussels.

Our staff are not converting to new technology fast enough.

We have too many staff and would like a painless and legal way of shedding some.

Each of the *Why?* questions, the reasons why we have a problem to solve in the first place, will lead us down a different path or *What?* and each *What?* will require a different *How?* and so on. In any successful meeting the questioning *Why?* activities have to be completed to a satisfactory level before we move onto the *What?* analysis, and so on. The Questioning Stage requires the asking of open questions, non-politically controlled discussion, trust, *time* . . .

------------➤

EXERCISE

Consider the stages of the meeting – the *Why?* questioning stage, the *What?* analysis stage, the *How?* practicality stage and the *'If'* action stage and list what sort of activities need to be accomplished.

What sort of states of mind would need to be encouraged in each stage and how could these states be encouraged in any real organisation?

Stages of a Meeting

What needs to be done for - Why? - What? - How? - If?

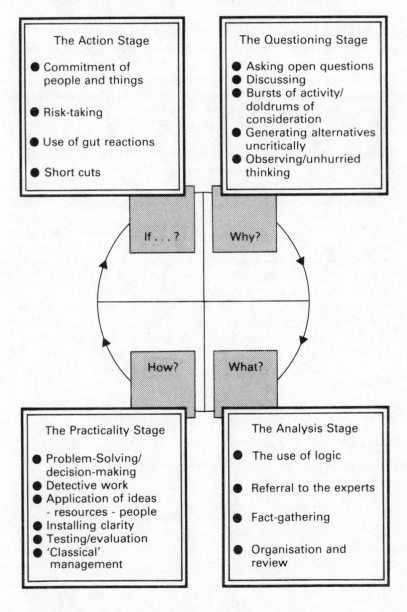

The Action Stage

- Commitment of people and things

- Risk-taking

- Use of gut reactions

- Short cuts

The Questioning Stage

- Asking open questions
- Discussing
- Bursts of activity/ doldrums of consideration
- Generating alternatives uncritically
- Observing/unhurried thinking

If . . .?   Why?

How?   What?

The Practicality Stage

- Problem-Solving/ decision-making
- Detective work
- Application of ideas - resources - people
- Installing clarity
- Testing/evaluation
- 'Classical' management

The Analysis Stage

- The use of logic

- Referral to the experts

- Fact-gathering

- Organisation and review

For the *Why?* or Questioning Stage of a meeting there is likely to be a great deal of speculation and fuzzy ideas. People are inclined to move into bursts of activity followed by complete blockages and the process is not subject to tight management control. The state of mind most preferred in the Questioning Stage needs Natural Child and techniques such as Brainstorming can encourage this in the most staid people. The Questioning Stage is one that people who value the use of their Natural Child enjoy most and in organisations where Natural Children are not welcome the *Why?* stage is often either assumed or ignored. The Natural Child speculation is brought into logical control by the Adult behaviour of the *What?* – Analysis Stage. Here facts are collected to substantiate the speculations and 'experts' are brought in. We begin to organise and review. In the Kepner Tregoe System we rigorously collate and weight all our objectives and then compare on a numerical scale how the possible alternatives measure up to them.

Once we have done all the Adult work of the Analysis Stage we need to move on and ask the Critical Parent questions of whether certain things are practical in a real world. We need to ask *How?* in the third stage, and here we want no fuzzy concepts – decisions have to be made and real resources utilised. 'Classical' managers with strong, effective and valued Critical Parents are in their element. The Practical Stage can be helped by following the Kepner Tregoe process and some of the other decision-making systems ranging from the sophisticated computer-aided methods to simple structuring techniques. The final stage – the *'If'* – Action Stage of the meeting goes beyond decisions and *does things*. Resources, including people, are committed and risks are taken:

'It's a bit late for that now . . .'

'OK, I know it would be nice but . . .'

'I had to take a flier . . . it felt right and we need it *now*.'

The techniques for the Action Stage include – GANTT charts, Critical Paths, Research Planning Diagrams . . . The managers who most enjoy the Action state usually value their Little Professors.

→

EXERCISE

Consider a Problem-Solving meeting you have attended in your organisation.

Were all the stages represented?

What would you see as the predominant state of mind of the meeting?

On the whole, what stage would you see as being most important for the process of solving the particular problem on hand?

⟶

Barbara Carlsson working for Procter & Gamble in the USA considers that any project goes several times round our *Why – What – How – 'If'* cycle before it is completed – from concept to realisation and that the meetings organised round the project also show this emphasis. We would certainly see that although we do need to ask *Why?* in any problem-solving situation, the emphasis on the Questioning Stage is likely to be towards the concept stage of any project and the emphasis on analysis will be in the research stage. The testing and building stage will emphasise practicalities and the 'marketing' stage, in whatever sense, will concentrate efforts in the Action Stage. However, all organisations need to concern themselves with all the stages, some of the time.

The British Central Clearing Banks have recently suffered a considerable shock against the onslaught of the Building Societies. The problem, using our model of organisational behaviour – *Why?* – *What?* – *How?* – *'If?'* was probably that the banks had concentrated their efforts on the *What?* and *How?* questions. People with valued skills in analysis and practicality got to the top of the organisations and recruited in their own images. We will say more about this in the next chapter.

Organisations who have a deficiency in the ability to ask *Why?* questions get better and better at the same things but lose the ability to change. The *Why?* questioning process has the function of the look-out on board a ship – most of the time it is not needed but without it you do not notice the unexpected iceberg ahead. The Try Hard sub-themes of mind music block out the ability to stand back and think – to ask *Why?*

The stages of problem-solving in meetings

	Questioning Why?	Analysis What?	Practicality How?	Action 'If?'
PURPOSE OF STAGE	Generating alternatives Recognising problems	Formulating theories Defining problems	Testing theories Solving problems	Committing and implementing
TOO LITTLE	Blind	Silly	No focus	Late
RIGHT BALANCE	Creative	Sound	Clear	Achieving
TOO MUCH	Paralysed by ideas	Boring/ impractical	Rigid	Wild
TOOLS	Brainstorming Browsing Reading Time	Thinking Experts Data bases Theory	Decision systems Experiments Calculations	'Time Management' Planning/ Scheduling

But as we have said, there are three factors at the problem-solving meeting – the people, the problem and the methodology/process. For instance some problems virtually *demand* an analytical approach, while others defy any other approach than the strictly 'suck-it-and-see' action approach. Certain ranges of techniques fit these approaches but more importantly certain people value their skills most in certain areas – there are Action Managers, and Practical Managers. Let's discuss this in the next chapter.

CHAPTER SIX

Sector People

'I have to deal with lots of specialists – instructing, praising and blaming and of course supervising the work. Obviously they need to be treated differently – is there some sort of guideline?'

'How do I give my boss bad news?'

'I find that I either warm to people within the first few seconds of an interview or not.'

'One problem we meet is that the whole department seems to be cloned. The other problem is that when we have to find someone who is different we seem to use the method of sticking in a pin. We have made some horrendous mistakes.'

Just as Taibi Kahler and Ellis were able to show patterns in what we have termed Mind Music, there also appear to be patterns in 'Valued Skills'. This chapter is about these patterns and how they can be understood and used by the Aware Manager to work more effectively with the human diversity he or she finds in the workplace. We will begin where we left off in the previous chapter – the effective problem-solving meeting and look back at the four quadrants of the process – the Questioning Stage, the Analysis Stage, the Practical Stage and the Action Stage. We are extending the concept. We see management as one vast extended problem-solving exercise and the stages we have discussed before in a limited context are the stages of our work as managers. The total process is of course cyclic, each answer bringing in its turn new questions. We mentioned, almost in passing, that people preferred and were more effective in, particular quadrants. As people we will call them after the quadrants – the *Why?* people, the *What?* people, the *How?* people and the *'If?'* people, but when we discuss them as managers we need to look at their management and name them accordingly. Thus the *Why?* people as managers find that their valued skills cluster in the Questioning

Stage and hence develop their jobs in this direction and they are perceived as Questioning Managers – we shall find a more professional sounding title later. Such managers have a recognisable style or personality – they look after their people and they value the skills of unhurried reflection. Other managers appear quite differently. The *What?* people as managers show a pattern of valued skills concerned with the application of logic and gathering data and shine in analysis seeing themselves as logical. They manage through the control of resources. The *How?* people see themselves as Practical Managers and their valued skills produce a very clear concept of management: 'The job of a manager is to manage.' They are the 'classical managers'.

Such practical managers function through the application of skills and honour skills that have a perceived utility very highly. They are impatient with what they perceive as the dreamers of the Questioning quadrant and are only concerned with the utility of the work of those functioning in the Analysis quadrant.

Our final group of people, the *'If?'* people function as Action folk who have to be doing something and can be quite unselective as to what that something is. Their valued skills are concerned with achieving the ends and they are less concerned with the means.

We can probably all work in all the four quadrants of problem-solving.

However, our valued skills are very often concentrated in one or two quadrants.

To derive personal satisfaction at work we manoeuvre our jobs to make most use of these valued skills and hence mould our preferred management style.

➤

EXERCISE

Look back into the book and at the case studies concerning Betty and Campbell – Chapter 1, Dennis our Marketing Executive in Chapter 3, and Harry Hamid, the manager who had problems with the football supporter in Chapter 4.

In which of the four quadrants – Questioning, Logical, Practical and Action – would you place Betty, Campbell, Dennis and Harry?

How would you see their perceptions of the management role differing? Attempt to put a title on their individual perceptions of 'the job of a manager'.

Henry, we would see as working from the Questioning quadrant – a *Why?* person. He would see his job as providing the facilities for his staff to accomplish their tasks. In talking to the process worker he was actually trying to help and he would see the personal growth of each and every member of his staff as important. When faced with the man who said he was sorry, he was able to see much more of the total picture than was to his own good. Managers operating predominantly from the Questioning quadrant are inclined to avoid conflict. They also have a habit, disturbing for the rest of us, of only knowing what they think after they have said it – they develop their ideas through others. Henry's detractors might find him uncritical, procrastinating and lacking in purpose. His many friends would find him creative and having the ability to see things in a true perspective, regardless of his own direct interests. He would see his role as that of a *facilitator* of those he managed and be proud of their personal development.

Dennis, our marketing executive, was a sound logical manager, except under stress – he was a *What?* person. He valued the use of his Adult to develop situations by analysis. He liked to be able to write things down and organise, to follow a plan and avoid emotions. He believed strongly in hierarchy and trusting the experts, bosses, etc. His downfall happened when the experts or the bosses did not fit his own theoretical map of how people should behave. Dennis would have colleagues who found him slow to react, always wanting to check and 'be sure'. He would be seen as being over-cautious and failing to recognise the human factors in himself and his colleagues – he would be the last to acknowledge himself or anyone else as a victim of stress. His staff might also find him privately rather boring and cold. His friends, for whom caution was not a criticism, would find him organised and able to work effectively without having to have people

Styles of Management

Manager's valued questions - Why? - What? - How? - If?

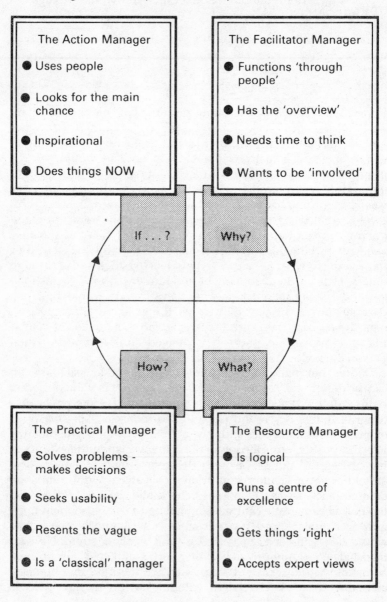

helping him. He would be professionally helpful and a fount of experience. His department would be run so as to be a centre of excellence and he would defend his staff like a tiger its cubs. His library would contain the significant books of his expert skill, written by the gurus of the trade. We would see him defining his role as that of a *Resource Manager*.

Campbell was a *How?* person acting as a *Practical Manager* who used judgement to achieve his goals. He liked to be in charge of the situation and learned by testing and checking against recognised criteria. His values were those of clarity and sturdiness and he profoundly objected to those who betrayed the 'old-fashioned values' of loyalty and service. His friends would see him as a pillar of common sense and his staff would find him loyal and fair – 'you know where you are with Campbell'. His detractors would see him as being bigoted and as undervaluing personal feeling – his own and his staff's. They might also see him as over-influenced by qualifications and perhaps a great user of what used to be called 'the Birmingham screwdriver' – a hammer – in situations where all the facts did not fit a black and white picture. Colleagues and staff might also resent his authoritarian attitudes and his impatience with people and ideas when they lacked clarity.

Betty, our *'If?'* person, comes over as an *Action Manager* of quadrant four. She would take risks, derive a considerable satisfaction in involving others and pride herself on her ability to think on her feet. We can almost hear her say:

'Well you win some, you lose some.'

As a people manager she would lead from the front and have a complete disregard for those who did not follow. I have a concept of the posthumous VCs from the World Wars acting something like Betty. Betty would not be a loyal manager to her staff and her concept of appraisal would be that of 'weeding'. Betty would judge herself by actual achievements – products on the shelf. Her detractors would see her as disorganised, impulsive and having too many irons in the fire to be real. They might also grant her a grudging respect but not seek out her company or opinions. She would be demanding of her colleagues and friends and almost dismissive of her own mistakes. Her many social friends and admirers, however, could well see her as inspired and excellent company.

———————▶

EXERCISE

Look back at your own valued skills and see how much you fit
into the four categories.

It is unlikely that you fit exactly into any one profile but I
suspect that you would find one of our quartet – Henry,
Dennis, Campbell or Betty – a more rewarding companion than
the others.

Now look again at your X and Y scores. Accepting that the X
scores probably represent your *natural* style of management –
what does the movement to the Y scores suggest?

                                                  ———————▶

You Tell Them

A large part of the management job consists of instructing people
to do things. It will come as no surprise to you the reader, that
the understanding of yourself and the other person is very
important for effective verbal management communication. We
are not all the same and do not function at our best if we are
treated as if we were alike. Someone working in the Questioning
quadrant of Problem-Solving, either because this is the most
appropriate stage to be in or because this is where their valued
skills predominate, will have a great deal of energy in the Child
states of mind, and the issue is – How do we communicate
effectively with people in the Child states? Someone working
in, by nature or pressure, the Analysis quadrant will have
energies predominant in Adult – how do we communicate with
a predominantly Adult state of mind? The Practical quadrant
demands Critical Parent to predominate and the Action quadrant
is probably dominated by the Little Professor – how does one
communicate with peers, subordinates or even bosses who
operate chiefly from Critical Parent or Little Professor?

There are five lines of management communication:

Child to Child   – EMOTIVE

Nurturing Parent to Adapted Child   – NURTURATIVE

Adult to Adult	– LOGICAL
Critical Parent to Adult	– DIRECTIVE
and	
Critical Parent to Adapted Child	– INTERRUPTIVE

———————▶

EXERCISE

Tell a subordinate that his or her car is in the way and needs to be moved in each of the first four channels of management communication.

Why have we not included the fifth channel in the exercise?

Which of the channels would you see as most appropriate for Henry, Dennis, Campbell and Betty in similar circumstances?

———————▶

We often use this exercise with a group of say five managers. Each is given a marked piece of paper – one for each of the four channels and one a blank. The manager drawing the blank is given instructions by the other four and he or she has to guess the channel by recognising the words, tones and gestures of the sender. Very often we find that people are blocked from using one of the channels and that managers who have identified disciplinary problems use too complex forms of words for simple instructions.

KEEP IT SIMPLE
KNOW WHAT YOU WANT
EXPECT TO BE OBEYED

Examples of the instructions to move the car have included:

The **Emotive** Channel – Child to Child

'Move that rust bucket.' The words are said with a smile.

The **Nurturative** Channel – Nurturing Parent to Adapted Child

'If I were you I would move your car. It's quite likely to get damaged over there.'

The **Logic** Channel – Adult to Adult

'Your car is in a very dangerous place and could well cause an accident.'

The **Directive** Channel – Critical Parent to Adult

'I am the Safety Officer and I have to tell you to move your car immediately.'

The Interruptive Channel would differ from the Directive Channel in that no reason or authority need be given:

'Move your car *now!*'

The stance of the Directive Channel manager would be firm, with eye contact. The Interruptive Channel sender could well avoid direct eye contact – looking over a pile of papers or down through eyebrows and turn away immediately after the order.

Why is the Interruptive Channel not on our 'recommended list'? The answer is partly in the way it can be accepted – there is *no* recovery if the Interruptive Channel is not accepted. If the Adapted Child in the recipient is not available and transfers the 'call' to his or her Critical Parent or Rebellious Child – we have trouble.

'Who are you to give me orders?' or 'Go to hell!' What do we do then? Do we want to risk a disciplinary procedure arising from a minor car-parking misdemeanour?

Remember the Head Teacher from the second chapter who suddenly understood the variety of responses he had when he used his Critical Parent on 'little people' and expected a compliant Adapted Child – so it is with managers. Your Critical Parent expecting a compliant Adapted Child will trigger an ancient response and it may not be what you want.

So, accepting that the *Why?* person is operating predominantly from a Child state of mind, we would communicate using either the Emotive – Child to Child or the Nurturative – Nurturing Parent to Adapted Child channels. Our example Henry could well go into 'big persons' forms of the sulks if we showed much of our Critical Parent. Our *What?* logical Dennis would require an Adult to Adult Logical Channel and would resent any sign of Nurturing Parent as us 'talking down to him'. He would in extreme accept Directive Critical Parent to Adult. Campbell, our Practical *How?* person has a great deal of Critical Parent and needs to have this held by anyone expecting to hold his interest. The Directive Channel – Critical Parent – is required and any sign of Child to Child Emotive or Nurturative, will be rejected. Adult to

Lines of Communication

Communications to those working primarily in one quadrant

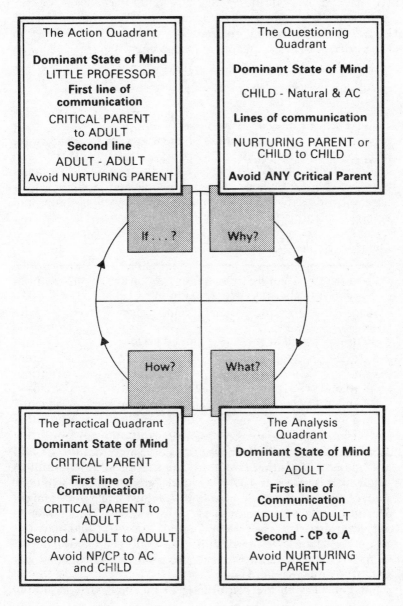

The Action Quadrant

Dominant State of Mind
LITTLE PROFESSOR
First line of communication
CRITICAL PARENT
to ADULT
Second line
ADULT - ADULT
Avoid NURTURING PARENT

The Questioning Quadrant

Dominant State of Mind

CHILD - Natural & AC

Lines of communication

NURTURING PARENT or CHILD to CHILD

Avoid ANY Critical Parent

If . . . ?   Why?

How?   What?

The Practical Quadrant
Dominant State of Mind
CRITICAL PARENT
First line of Communication
CRITICAL PARENT to ADULT
Second - ADULT to ADULT
Avoid NP/CP to AC and CHILD

The Analysis Quadrant
Dominant State of Mind
ADULT
First line of Communication
ADULT to ADULT
Second - CP to A
Avoid NURTURING PARENT

Adult will be acceptable provided he accepts that he is among peers. Betty, with her high Little Professor, needs to be told – Directive Critical Parent to Adult and told again. She is very able to manipulate any Child to Child or Nurturing Parent.

We have discussed the media for communication using the quadrants, but how about the message? Can we apply our knowledge of individual quadrants to improve our efficiency in the principal issues of people management:

ISSUING INSTRUCTIONS

APPRAISING – PRAISING AND BLAMING

SUPERVISING?

I would see the answer as being *yes*.

How would you brief, praise/blame and supervise Henry for instance? Henry values his skills in the Questioning quadrant and is interested in the *Why?* questions of the world. He works in bursts of energy. He is interested in people and facilitating their work. He prides himself on seeing the whole view of things and is forever wanting to know *Why?*

The simple rules are:

> Brief people from the previous sector to their valued sector
> Supervise in the succeeding quadrant
>
> IF THEY RESPECT YOUR VIEW:
>
> Praise or blame in their own valued sector
>
> IF THEY DO NOT RESPECT YOU OR YOUR RIGHT TO MANAGE THEM:
>
> as second best – praise or blame from your own valued sector
> Maintain the correct Channel of Communications always.

Let's try to apply the rules for Henry. Firstly *ALL* our communications would be in his favoured lines of communication – Child to Child and Nurturing Parent to Child. We could use Adult to Adult to less effect and *ANY* Critical Parent must be avoided. Henry can easily be made to go into Adapted Child and it might be said that his very creativity is his own way of responding to the world so that he has a place. Henry's Adapted Child may well become rebellious and he will sulk. The Critical Parent dominated manager – the Practical Manager from our classification – will have trouble managing Henry.

Let's go back to the disciplining of the process worker. We

MANAGING USING THE QUADRANTS

Briefing - Praising/Appraising/Supervising

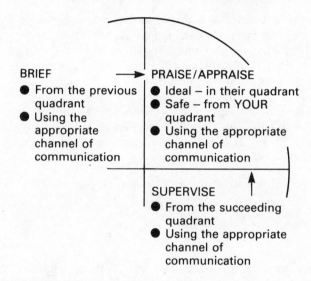

BRIEF ⟶ **PRAISE/APPRAISE**

- From the previous quadrant
- Using the appropriate channel of communication

- Ideal – in their quadrant
- Safe – from YOUR quadrant
- Using the appropriate channel of communication

SUPERVISE

- From the succeeding quadrant
- Using the appropriate channel of communication

would brief Henry from the preceding quadrant to which he is operating or prefers to operate. In this case the Action *'If?'* quadrant.

'I am having a lot of trouble with the unions at the moment and it would help me a lot if you could take it from here.'

(Adapted Child to Adapted Child)

'Come on Henry, it's your turn – tell him.'

(Natural Child to Natural Child)

'Look Henry, if you miss this one you will lose all respect. I'll back you up if you have trouble but *you* have to do it.'

(Nurturing Parent to Adapted Child)

I imagine such 'instructions' will be uncomfortable for the Practical Managers reading the book.

Let's look at supervising Henry. Here we are working from the succeeding quadrant – the Logical *What?* quadrant, we need to understand exactly what Henry has done. Henry in his dealing with the process worker in Chapter 4 knew exactly why he was doing the job but exactly what he did was completely different. This is where he needs supervising.

'I need to get this straight Henry so we know where we are. What exactly was said? Did you issue the verbal warning? It makes quite a difference.'

(with the correct gestures – Adapted Child to Adapted Child)

Because it is difficult to exercise control through Adapted Child such a request is very weak. It may well have to be the subject of a Broken Record. We may have to persist.

The Nurturing Parent to Adapted Child might well be more appropriate and more comfortable:

For all our sakes Henry I have to get it straight . . .'

In praising or blaming Henry we need to look at our own relationship with him. If he does respect our views he will accept Praise or Blame in his own quadrant – the Questioning *Why?* quadrant:

'I liked the sensitive way you dealt with that situation Henry.'

(Nurturing Parent to Adapted Child)

'That was absolutely evil Henry. Everyone is in a mess now.'

(Child to Child)

If Henry does not respect us as a person or our right to manage him then it is safer to work from our own quadrant. The alternative is to risk sounding patronising.

Thus as Henry's manager, the Resource Manager from the Analysis quadrant would praise or blame on the basis of what has been done, the Practical Manager on the methodology and the Action Manager on the effects. As second best, working from the sender of the messages quadrant would still be effective:

'That must have been difficult but you stuck to the book.'

'I like the way you got all the relevant data to your elbow before you began the interview. It was well done.' . . . or of course the opposite.

The Action Manager would either catch Henry's jacket and say: 'Great, we won't have trouble with him again,' or ignore Henry for the rest of the time.

———————▶

EXERCISE

Using our rules how would you brief, praise/blame and super-vise, Dennis, Campbell and Betty?

Take individuals from your own teams and make a judgement as to what quadrant they are predominantly working from.

Take a real situation and devise forms of words and gestures that will effectively brief, praise/blame and supervise each.

Would you be comfortable with such approaches and do they make sense to you?

———————➤

Dennis, when not under stress, responds most effectively to Adult to Adult communication and for his briefing needs to be told *why* he has to do something:

'The customer is complaining and we need to keep the contract. I leave what is done to you.'

This would have allowed him space to use his valued skills of analysis and do things in an effective way. In being *told* how things had to be done, Dennis would be, and was in our example, panicked.

We would supervise Dennis on how he was doing the job:

'Are you going out yourself or . . .' and praise/blame him on what he had done:

'The detailed analysis on the Malaysian work was superb.'

'You made a mistake.'

Even a hint of Nurturing Parent will be seen as patronising to Dennis.

Campbell, our third quadrant *How?* Practical Manager, needs to be told exactly what needs to be done – he needs a specification and his line of communication is one of authority – Critical Parent to Adult.

'The objective of the reorganisation is to reduce waste in the second stage of manufacture.

The product comes from the first stage at a price of £30 a kilo and at the completion of the second stage at £100 a kilo. Your brief is to make sure that errors are recognised before any processing happens in Stage 2.'

Boring perhaps to the non-Practical Managers reading this book but such directive and detailed instructions will provide Campbell with free run on *how* to solve the problems – the set of skills he personally values using. What, however, he actually does may have consequences for the rest of the plant and this needs to be supervised – the *'if'* bit:

'I need to see exactly how you plan to do the exercise so that I can make sure that we do not tread on anyone's feet.'

Campbell is very easy to praise/blame:

'A job well done.'

'Your behaviour/work was not up to the standards of the profession.'

The Practical Managers I have known were not too good at accepting criticism of any kind, so anyone attempting really well-directed adverse criticism had better be very careful.

Betty can also be a problem as a subordinate. One characteristic of the Action Manager is a very short attention span and they have to be virtually nailed to the floor when being given instructions. All the time you are giving the brief they will be working out all the angles and vanishing into their own little worlds.

'Betty, this is going to take some time so I have arranged for all calls to be taken by Pat. I want you to do a study of communications in the complex. There are about 1,000 people employed and I want a survey of half – 500 of them over the next two weeks . . .' and closing with . . . 'I would like you to send me a plan with all the times and costs by the end of the week – you know, exactly what you intend to do.'

However well you brief Betty she will do it her way and the supervision needs to be in the *Why?* quadrant – you have to remember why the job was set in the first place and make sure that *exactly* what she does fits those objectives, working all the time from the Critical Parent to what you can find as her Adult. She will manipulate any sign of Nurturing Parent.

'I need to be clear. I think using the telephone was very creative but I have a concern that it may not meet our prime objective. The very people we are most interested in are likely to be living in digs and have no access to phones.'

Praise or blame for Betty is easy – in her own Action quadrant:

'The results were excellent and you will see the results in the shops in due time.'

'You failed.'

EXERCISE

Imagine the following situation.

You have been given clear and direct instructions to complete a particular task within set time constraints. You understand what is required of you and the job is well within your abilities but you are not happy. Something – a pump is making the wrong noises, a contractor looks shaky, a computer system is throwing up error messages . . . You feel that there is a better than fifty-fifty chance of a complete and lengthy failure *unless* immediate action is taken. The action, a shutdown/delay will put the project back weeks but the gamble to carry on could cost the project maybe a year's delay and you believe this.

How do you tell your boss? Take a boss in each of the four quadrants and work out *exactly* how you would get over the information, the time, the place and the channel. Remember the message is part brief, part supervision and part motivation.

Using this exercise with managers from many backgrounds and over several years we have come up with many ideas, and a number of people who expect us to come up with a magic formula. The key is to *avoid your boss's valued quadrant*. Lead him or her into the quadrant but let them work in their own valued quadrant by themselves. Offer help *when asked* but do not crowd. Use the correct channel of communication.

The *Why?* Facilitator Manager will be slow to respond and will take his or her time. Any form of pushing will be counter-productive. The best advice we have come up with is to explain the consequences, face to face – come from the *'If?'* quadrant and be available to answer questions.

'I feel that we may have a problem (Adapted Child) and that if we don't face it things could get out of hand.'

The contact has to be one-to-one and in private. *No* written report should be prepared and you need to hope that your boss will come back *asking* for your Nurturing Parent:

'What do you suggest?'

A detailed proposal will be seen as Critical Parent and may well lose you your case.

The logical *What?* Resource Manager will require a case – *why* he needs to be concerned. He or she will see any analysis as a challenge to their authority:

'I have a picture here of problems – and according to the Chief Engineer he will not guarantee the pump. If it fails we have real trouble. Some seven or eight months delay while we strip down and get a new system. That could lose us the market.'

'Fine, get the data on the previous installation and . . .'

Once your manager begins to ask *you* questions you have done the best in the circumstances.

The Practical *How?* Manager needs to know the facts. We would see that a written report should be available and that a formal interview should be requested:

'Thank you for seeing me. In the report you will notice that the pump is now using three pints of lubricant a shift. Our previous experience is that it only needed routine topping up. We have measured the . . .'

Your manager may question the facts and *clear* the decision with you, but that is the most you can expect. Under no circumstances do you presume to tell him or her what to do. Decision-making is a valued skill of the *How?* quadrant.

The *'If?'* Action Manager needs to know what you feel ought to be done and that has to be face-to-face. You will either be believed or not and the action will be immediate:

'What are you suggesting – close it down – can/cannot be done old thing. Risk it.' Or '. . . close it.'

We wish you luck in the greatest skill any aware manager could possess – living productively with one's boss.

Yes But I Have Them All in My Team – And They Change under Pressure.

Let's look at the massive shifts of states of mind that some of us have under pressure first. We do not see the revised set of states of mind corresponding to a new set of values or indeed a true management style. The move unwatched corresponds to what several writers called the WIB style – a Weak Inconsistent Bastard. It is up to us to check and review our own pressures and allow our subordinates to do the same.

'Look, these are the people I have to work with.'

If all four quadrants are present in a team, unless things are rigorously structured, they will all be tripping over each other in their attempts to use their valued skills.

'I need a few minutes to think that one out.'

'The information we have now is simply not adequate to decide anything.'

'I think that any more data will actually fog the issue. What we need now is a clear decision.'

'Let me know when you characters have finished!'

The techniques of Brainstorming, Kepner Tregoe Analysis, Gannt charts, etc., will force most people to work in a relevant stage of any actual problem-solving process, but the techniques do not always succeed and they certainly do not work over extended periods. The leopard finds its spots.

The issue is that of the mind music in our heads. The strongly practical manager at a Brainstorming session designed to emphasise the Questioning stage of the problem-solving process may well have difficulties silencing his or her Be Strong sub-themes:

'This is all fuzzy rubbish. How can sensible people sit seriously round a table and put up ideas like that. There are so many things that I ought to be doing.'

And the action folk could well be deafened by their Hurry Up sub-themes:

'That's a great idea. What I would need is a bit of space and we could actually try it. Costing would be a problem but . . .'

I was running a Brainstorming session for a group of managers from the old Walls Meat Company on the subject of selling more sausages. About the fifth idea to appear on the flip charts was concerned with the concept of selling mustard. The rather wild connection was that Colman's Mustard sells more mustard to be wasted on the plate than to be eaten – could you sell sausages in the same way?

A marketing manager of Walls got up suddenly, located a phone at the corner of the room and was speaking to a friend in Colman's Mustard and the meeting finished in confusion after ten minutes. The advertising campaign – with Colmans – showing a beautifully cooked sausage on a plate with mustard was on the hoarding in an amazingly short time, and was effective.

The other non-Action managers at the meeting felt cheated and acted annoyed.

We can speculate on the Analytical *What?* person having a Be Perfect sub-theme and the Questioning *Why?* person a strong Please Me sub-theme and begin to understand how it is we can clone our friends and associates. *What?* people for instance think and feel alike and are comfortable in each other's company. In interviews *What?* people answer questions in a predictable way and are the very people that other *What?* people find it is easy to warm to. The very opposite is true, *What?* people with their tendency to Be Perfect sub-themes and a wish to organise and establish order, can well be driven into panic by the '*If?*' people and their Hurry Up.

Many people can have their valued skills clustered into four sets:

the *Why?*, the *What?*, the *How?*, and the *If?* person

In choosing colleagues and friends our views may well be dominated by whether 'by nature' we are a *Why?*, a *What?*, a *How?* or an *If?* Person.

The choice may be for an easy life – 'our sort' or for excitement, in either case our choice is not rational.

Bob Sample, an American psychologist, author and educationalist, tells the story of some work he did for interest among his friends. Using a psychometric test devised by David Kolb and Bernice

McCarthy to look at the personality profiles of married couples, he
came up with the startling conclusion:

'On the whole people seem to marry in opposing quadrants [*What?*
to *'If?'* . . .] for the first marriage and in the same quadrant – like
to like – for the second marriage. *This does not mean that the second
marriage is more successful, only that the rows are different.'*

The issues of communication between the four classifications of
managers can be considerable even in the limited time-span of a
meeting but in the context of the whole management job, cannot
be over-emphasised. It is these communications issues that are
the basis of the rest of this chapter.

Valued stage of problem solving	Preferred state of mind	Valued concept of management	Likely mind music sub-theme	Stereotyped function
Questioning *why?*	Natural Child	Facilitating	Please Me	Personnel Corporate planning
Analysis *What?*	Adult	Resource Management	Be Perfect	R&D Accounts Computing
Practical *How?*	Parent	Practical down to earth	Be Strong/ Try Hard	Production
Action *'If?'*	Little Professor	Crisis	Hurry Up	Action-centred jobs

Getting The Right Person For The Job –
Selection Interviews

We are not trying to make a point that taking on an employee or
colleague is like getting married – although the thought had
crossed our minds. What we are trying to say is that a selection
interview needs to be as free of mind music as possible. In
practice many of us make up our minds in an interview within
the first few seconds and spend the rest of the time confirming
or denying our prejudices, and how do we avoid that? Well,

understanding the sort of person *we* are helps. What is our mind music? What valued concept of management do we have? We then need to understand what has to be achieved in the job – *not how we would do it*:

> Probably the most difficult issue of management is understanding the difference between a job done badly and a job not done the way you would have done it.

We need to be able to assess the other person – what is their likely mind music, what is likely to be their valued concept of management . . . overall are they a *Why?*, *What?*, *How?* or an *'If?'* person, not to judge them but to understand some of the things that will happen in the discussion.

> We were working on succession planning for a large engineering group and the Quality Assurance Director allowed us to interview him to illustrate our point. In a psychometric test he had proved an extreme *How?* person, as have nearly all the effective engineers we have ever met.
>
> 'Why did you take up Quality Assurance in the first place?'
>
> 'My own skills allow me to relate to the way it is done in the organisation. Nowadays we use simulations but in the old days the actual engines would be tested . . .'
>
> 'What has to be done to the engines if they fail?'
>
> 'The particular part is bypassed in the system and the rectification unit gives it more detailed tests using a larger simulation. Here we have gone off the micros and onto the main frame . . .'
>
> 'If too many engines fail in one period, what are the consequences for the customer?'
>
> 'I have to fill in a series of chits and of course the customer gets some of these . . .'

As somebody with both *'If?'* and *Why?* valued skills myself I found the interview rather confusing. I thought I was asking *Why, What, How* and *'If'* questions and all the time he was telling me *how* it was done. I wanted to know about consequences to the customer and he was giving me detail on *how* the customer was being told. I asked him *why* he took on the job and he gave me a history lesson on *how* it was and is done. He blossomed when I actually asked him a *How?* question and could have gone on for hours. If I had been a *How?* person myself, the dialogue would have been exciting for both of us. But I am not and I found it confusing.

As an interviewer for real, what would have been the effect? How did the interview go? Well it depends on who *you* are. If you had been a *how* person you would have warmed to the *how* answers and, other things being equal, our friend would have got the job. I feel quite strongly that a *why* person would have felt that the interviewee was evading the question, that an *'If '* person would have got bored and probably the *What* person would have seen him in terms of a tool that could get the department working.

THE EFFECTIVE INTERVIEW

1   Know what is required as skills for the job and check them in the applicant.
2   Understand yourself – your valued skills.
3   With or without a psychometric test, interview by asking *Why*, *What*, *How* and *'If'* questions.
4   Check the energy of the responses in each quadrant.
5   Balance how you feel the applicant would develop the job to use his or her valued skills against how you feel comfortable about the job being done.

EXERCISE

If you are concerned with selection procedures, on the whole are you satisfied with their efficiency – do you get the right people into the right jobs within a reasonable space of time and cost?

Think of a selection interview situation in your recent past. How was it conducted and was the decision made rationally?

Could using the methodology described have helped develop a more effective process?

The dimensions of what is loosely and variously known as

Leadership Style, Management Style and Styles of Decision-Making have worried the author quite a lot and before we proceed to the next chapter, some clarification is necessary.

We see the term Leadership Style as coming from a machismo view of management. Manager the Leader – useful as an image when appropriate but restricted in that many effective managers would never see their roles as Leader. An effective manager can facilitate or resource allocate and the leadership, such as it is, can come from elsewhere. Management Style has two elements – that which is our preferred style using our valued skills to what we perceive as their best advantage and a situationally dependent style. The situationally dependent style of management will be the topic of the next chapter. Here we will be saying that in any management situation involving problem-solving or decision-making the manager is not truly a free agent and is unwise to adopt his or her preferred style of management without careful consideration. Thus a Facilitator manager might well *prefer* to handle a management problem by getting all his or her staff together and discussing options. We could all think of many problems when this preferred style would be less than effective – manning a lifeboat for instance. Is there such a thing as a *best* style of management in a particular set of circumstances and if there is, what are the factors we need to look at to find it? It's a matter of style.

CHAPTER SEVEN

A Matter of Style – Situational Management

'I tell them, they don't do it and I worry about it.'

'It's talk, talk, talk, nobody seems to want to get on with the work.'

'I often wonder whether I am the right person for the job.'

In the last chapters we have made some useful generalisations about working with motivated and effective individuals. We accepted that different types of people might welcome different styles of communication from their managers and the channels of communications we mentioned were:

Directive – Standard-setting Critical Parent
Nurturative – Caring Parent addressing the Adapted Child state of mind
Logical – Adult communicating directly with another Adult
Emotive – Child addressing Child

We have mentioned a fifth channel of communication:

Interruptive – Raw Critical Parent demanding the attention of an Adapted Child in the recipient

but its use, in most circumstances, is likely to be counter-productive and we discussed a Head Teacher who found himself confused by the responses of pupils when he used it.

We also showed that many important tasks in managerial communication – instruction-giving, praising/blaming and super-vision, are also better achieved by understanding the valued or working quadrant of the recipient. Thus a highly motivated and sensible individual, and in this context we discussed Dennis, our marketing executive, would communicate best, when not under pressure, in Adult and when it was explained to him logically *why* the work had to be done, *what* was well or badly done and supervised by analysis of *how* he had gone about the work. The generalities of improved managerial communication fall down when we cannot assume that the subordinates, or indeed peers or bosses, are either fully motivated or competent. Our own position with respect to the whole situation also needs to be considered. The current chapter will look at what we will call *Situational Leadership* and how the method of managing a particular situation can be reviewed by the Aware Manager with his or her Adult state of mind clearly in the control seat.

Meryl Richardson, with a stroke of creative genius, discovered that he could market the waxy waste product from petroleum refining in little bottles and by adding Mentol could sell it as Vicks Vapour Rub. Feeling that other managers could well benefit from his entrepreneurial approach, he used some of his profits to set up centres for the study of managerial decision-making in North Carolina, USA. The Center for Creative Leadership, as he called it, as part of its work to improve European and American management, made a study of some sixty actual leadership decisions in US industry and followed the decisions and their implementation from conception to completion – and in some cases, to their failure. The study was conducted by Vic Vroom and Philip Yetton in the mid 1970s and was published in part in the *Journal* of the American Management Association, from which we will now be drawing parts of this chapter. In the study, Vic Vroom developed a classification of styles and management decision-making and related these styles to situations for which they are most applicable. Vic is relatively non-judgmental in his description of how individuals may choose to use the styles of management decision-making at their command and how the choice of decision-making method is part of a balance between a number of factors, one of which is the development of the team. His overall message is that by understanding that managers do have a choice of how they approach a particular situation and with this understanding and a set of very clear questions in your head, you may well work much more effectively in areas where mistakes can be personally very damaging. The original language Vic used was not exactly that used in either of our books, but it has considerable overlap and I hope he will forgive me for the 'translation'.

TYPES OF MANAGEMENT DECISION-MAKING

AI   The individual manager solves the problem or makes the decision using the information available at the time.

AII   The individual manager collects the relevant information from subordinate(s) and then decides on a solution or makes the decision. The manager may or may not choose to tell the subordinates about the nature of the problem while he or she is collecting the information. The subordinates act as a data source and not in any way as decision-makers.

Both AI and AII are from either of the Parent states of mind and we have called them Directive or Nurturative. AI and AII would not, on the whole be effective for dealing with people from the Logical second quadrant.

CI   The manager shares the problem with relevant subordinates individually, without getting them together in a group but telling them that he or she will make a considered decision which may or may not reflect individual advice.

CII   The manager shares the problem with relevant subordinates in a group but as in CI, explaining that the decision may or may not reflect the suggestions and views collected.

Again we have a Directive channel but unlike the AI/AII there is unlikely to be a risk of Critical Parent to Adapted Child. The CI/CII style would stand more chance with the Logical second quadrant people than the AI/AII.

GI   The manager acts as non-directive counsellor to an individual subordinate getting him or her to work out for themselves a solution to a problem which is personal to them and has minimal impact on other individuals or the organisation.

GII   The manager shares a problem with subordinates in a group and gives them formal permission to develop alternatives and if possible reach a consensus on what needs to be done. The manager may or may not take on the role of Chairperson at the meeting or meetings of the group but makes it clear that he or she will accept and implement any decision or solution that has the support of the whole group.

On the whole we would see this as a Logical channel – Adult speaking to Adult and as being preferred, by the sector two people.

———————▶

EXERCISE

Imagine you are in the position of considering that all your subordinates could benefit from reading *The Aware Manager*.

Get the point over to your subordinates using each one of the Vroom Management Decision Styles – AI, AII, CI, CII, GI and GII.

(This is the last time we will discuss GI in this book, since its use in management is highly specialised and like the Interruptive Communication Channel, is not in general management practice.)

———————▶

In the AII style you may choose to use a bald 'telling' statement on the Directive Channel – CP to A:

'You will all read the book.'

or you may choose to soften the blow by some 'selling' using a little of the Nurturative Channel – NP to AC:

'You will all benefit from reading the book and good marks on the exam that I will set could well ensure your promotion.'

Equally, and still in AI, you could delegate the message, giving to some unfortunate:

'Get them to read the book.'

In AII, and the reader may well have cracked Vic Vroom's code – A, C and G stand for Authoritarian, Consultative and Group, respectively with I and II indicating individual and several – we need to collect information before the instruction:

'Will everyone be in the office on Thursday? Fine, now get them together and . . .'

CI allows the subordinate some knowledge of what is to come:

'I am very keen on them all reading a book I found valuable. What sort of resistance are we likely to get if I tell them on Thursday? I need to make up my mind how to proceed.'

The CII strategy could involve many of the same words as the CI but the words would of course be addressed to a meeting of the group. The whole group would have to share their views and the views be heard in public by us before we make up our minds.

The GII strategy could well be for us to table a problem the organisation has with what is seen as avoidable problems. You would then define the importance you give to some resolution. You might well table possible solutions including some form of training and the group might well adopt a common language – that of the book. Exactly how the group responds to the criticism, and respond it must, is not something you are going to tell them. However, if the group does come up with a legitimate, possible and agreed strategy to reduce future management mistakes, you will abide by and implement the recommendations. How much further you 'assist' in the group's decision-making process depends very much on individual style. Managers who are perceived as democratic may well be able to sit in for the group discussions and push their own point of view on a 'one person one vote' basis. Most manager will not be able to do this and would find that they always possessed at least 1.5 votes at the meeting. In using a GII style most of us would be advised to say something like:

> 'I must say again that I will abide by the decision and I'm going to leave you to it. Let me know when you have decided.'

The major mistake for any manager is to indicate a GII process and then not accept the GII recommendations of the group. A group is often flattered by being allowed a GII process and can be helped by the process to form a *team*. The new team will hit back if the manager 'betrays' it by reverting to control – A or C styles.

➤

EXERCISE

Think of a management decision you have been involved with in the recent past.

1   What of the AI and GII styles most accurately fits what you actually did?

2   Think how you could have used each of the styles and the consequences if you had –

Physically how could you have adopted the strategy?

How would you have felt?
What would have been the immediate consequences?
What would have been the long-term pay-off for the
organisation?

3   With hindsight, did you do right?

⟶

Hopefully your analysis of the exercise will allow you to look
differently at your own personal management decision-making
style. An example of such insight came when we were working
with one of the major UK clearing banks.

Case Study 1

In many banks throughout the world it is common for the manager
to have compulsory holiday periods for which another manager
covers the workings of the branch. The temporary branch manager
has the job of making sure that the branch is functioning as the
head office would wish. On the occasion we are remembering, the
temporary bank manager had recognised fraud and the head office
had taken action, part of the action being to install a peripatetic
manager to sort things out. The peripatetic manager had a clear
brief – 'Get the branch back on course.'

The natural inclination of the Head Office trouble-shooter was to
adopt a CII style but he soon found that this was impossible and
reverted to an AI which worked, but made him very happy to be
getting the train back to London when his mission had been
completed.

AI Style

Behaviour.   Sitting in the office and giving clear directives based
on Head Office protocol. No personal involvement with the staff.

Feelings and immediate consequences.   Isolation. The immediate
consequences were that he was hated but that discipline was
restored. Several 'problem' members of staff resigned after attempts
to justify had failed.

Long-term results.   The new manager acting as a permanent
replacement took over a working unit and was able to manage
appropriately.

AII was judged as impossible since there was certain complicity and nobody could be totally trusted.

CI Style

Behaviour.   He would have set up a series of private interviews with staff and taken note of comments.

Feelings and immediate consequences.   A feeling that everything was fair but somehow that he was being manipulated. The idea that *they* were fixing things.

Long-term results.   A long-lasting unofficial 'mafia' was set up for his successor to deal with.

CII Style

Behaviour.   Get them all together and sort it out.

Feelings and immediate consequences.   Should be the way to do it but somehow nobody is coming forward. A definite *me* against *them*.

Long-term results.   The cover-up is completed and probably *everyone* needs to find a new job.

GII Style

Behaviour.   Tell them they need to sort things out and to give a complete report.

Long-term results.   The investigator at least is looking for a job.

Some weeks before the manager completed the exercise he had been faced with the situation. He had chosen the CI route and found exactly what he explained in the exercise. He felt as if he was being told what an unofficial group wanted him to know and each of his private meetings was the subject of intense discussion in the canteen within minutes of its completion. He had moved rapidly to AI and in spite of feeling personally alienated, it had worked.

When you review your own exercise you may find such a shift. The key to effective management here is to make it very clear which style you are using – if you are actually in AI *never* give the idea that you are consulting. If you are really in CII be very careful that you indicate what you are doing and do not give the impression of GII. If CI/CII or GII does not work or cannot be completed in time and you have to move to AI/AII – explain carefully beforehand. A move from AI/AII to GII is virtually impossible.

⟶

EXERCISE

Look at the following case study and decide which of the styles AI to GII you would adopt. Make your decision quite rapidly and then ask yourself for the type of issues that made you decide.

Case Study 2: Attacking

The scene is from the World War Two book and film, *The Cruel Sea*. You are Captain Erickson and in command of a Corvette in the Battle of the Atlantic. Your sonar operator with your First Officer is advising you that a submarine is directly below a zone of water containing swimming survivors from a previously sunken merchantman. To chance the sinking of the U-Boat using the only weapons at your command – depth charges – will certainly kill the survivors. What style of management decision-making do you adopt?

⟶

The first point is that the progression from AI to GII is a movement from command to involvement. With an AI decision-making process, as perhaps we might recommend for Erickson RNR, the Captain takes all the responsibility for the decision, right or wrong. The issue is simple – will they do what he says and whether Erickson has enough data to make a valid decision. If Erickson knows enough to proceed and he is certain that his crew will obey, then he *can* choose AI. If he needs to check on the information and make sure that his First Officer is still certain of the signal from the U-Boat, then it has to be AII and in both the novel and the movie this is what happened. Erickson had to check that the information from the sonar was the best available and had not changed. He took an AII decision, which was to depth-charge the U-Boat regardless of his own feeling for the seamen in the water.

Why was Erickson so sure of his orders being obeyed?

The sources of power for anyone – manager or captain at war, are the same:

HIERARCHICAL OR LEGITIMATE
CREDIBILITY
EXPERT
CHARISMATIC

Erickson was certain he would be obeyed because he had all four sources of power: he had legitimate power, he was credible, he was *the* expert and he had the magic of charisma. His hierarchical power was vested by the Navy in his rank. As a Captain he could, if challenged, virtually keelhaul a mutineer. He was the Captain, he knew his ship and he had magic.

> The son of one of my colleagues has recently left officer training in the British Army as a Junior Officer and his first command was with a group who had completed two tours of duty in Northern Ireland, the last of which was under the command of an NCO. Taking over the group in Germany he technically had legitimate power to adopt an AI style of command but his credibility was such that he was wise enough to take AII decisions with his NCO for the first months – until he had won, and was seen to have won, his spurs.

Captain Erickson from *The Cruel Sea*, had expert power in that he, probably alone on the Corvette, *knew* how everything worked. He was there when the ship was laid down, fitted and commissioned and the Navy had been careful to keep him up-to-date in the changes of technology. He was *known* as the person most able to estimate the likelihood of an echo sounder being accurate, but even in the limits of the novel, his expert power base fades. In his final command – a Squadron of Frigates – he had had to acknowledge that the technology had grown away from him and that he was not fully acquainted with everything that went on. His level of command had been adjusted by the Navy so that his source of Hierarchical power was greater and his war record allowed him a greater credibility. This combined with his Charismatic power balanced his reduction in Expert power. The story of Erickson is happening to managers all over industry. A manager relying on expert sources of power will gradually find him or herself having to find new sources of power in virtually all areas of work and in particular the high technology industries. The legend has it that three months off the bench in the computer chip industry makes you struggle and a year turns you into a reminiscer.

What were other situational factors beyond Erickson's powerful hand of power sources, which made him virtually certain that the crew would obey?

Firstly, we would say that the crew had the same objectives as their 'manager' – U-Boat killing was their actual mission, and any differences they might have had in humanity were swamped by the total pressure of war. Having people with the same mission as you allows many industrial managers to take the short-cut of AI and AII.

We would like you to look at three further examples of managerial decision-making, perhaps much less cut and dried than the story of Erickson and hopefully nearer the world of the Aware Manager's everyday experience.

➡️

EXERCISE

Look at the next three case studies and decide what style of management decision-making you would adopt in similar situations. While you make your choice, think of the criteria you are using for your judgement.

Case Study 3: Just Parking

You are the new manager entrusted with the setting up of a small office with five subordinates – all of whom are of equal status. (Various ancillary workers supply functions such as cleaning but these are not the concern of the exercise.)

The office has been created out of two terraced houses backing onto a small cobbled street with jobbing garages and similar small businesses using the access. A public car park is readily accessible about 400 metres away and at a definite cost per day.

All your staff have cars and use them to get to work. All of them are recognised users of cars and claim normal company mileage rates.

Your issue is to arrange for car-parking at the office.

Case Study 4

You are the head of an R&D laboratory in the basic research department of a multinational. The programme of research in the laboratories has been arranged by your predecessor to all aspects of research – from 'blue skies' to service work. In your view the 'blue skies' work has evolved so that its commercial exploitation within the capability of the company is highly unlikely.

However, the skills of the 'blue skies' team are likely to be exactly what the company needs for some scientifically boring but commercially exciting projects that are appearing from the service work. The 'pure' research team are coherent and have a high morale. Their work is highly respected in the academic community and you are concerned that to get them to change goals to a less 'interesting' area, as indeed you must, will affect both their morale and their productivity.

The operating division requiring a shift in resources needs your laboratory's commitment within two weeks. The team could work on 'blue skies' projects as well as the strictly applied work but the effort of all of the team, even if only on a part-time basis, is necessary for success as far as the operating division, so total commitment is necessary from all members of the team. The choice of the actual 'pure' research projects still to be pursued in the new environment is also completely open and you do not have the expert skills to decide the priorities.

Get it settled.

Case Study 5

You are operations manager of an electronics company faced with major competition from the Pacific Basin. A programme of investment in automation has not come up with the reduction in manufacturing cost that was either demanded or expected – quality has fallen and key workers continue to leave.

To the limit of your knowledge in the industry as it is now, the systems you have installed are not defective but you do suspect that the working procedures that the robotics equipment has demanded are not ideal. This view is not shared by your immediate subordinates or indeed the shop floor. The popular view is that the training given to operatives combined with the confusion on bonus payments has led to poor morale and hence avoidable mistakes.

The situation has now come to a head and your divisional director is asking for a response by 12.00 to the recorded fall in profitability of your unit over the past six months. The director has confidence in you and will accept your views; however, he does need concrete plans from your division to present to the board meeting at 13.00.

Give him those plans.

The first case study was concerned with parking and perhaps the manager concerned may have had recollections of interminable disputes on this and similar 'trivial' issues in the past. Parkinson, of Parkinson's Law fame, talked about the Bicycle Shed case when a board meeting spent hours discussing the future of a cycle shed and only minutes on the expense of a new atomic power plant. What matters is that the issue is settled and that a decision sticks. The group of managers does not truly share the same goals as the manager and there is rivalry between them. The manager *could* use all his or her clout to enforce a decision, but then would have to continue to monitor the result for ever:

> 'Yes of course I know the rules but I had a particularly important client, load of heavy material, bad weather conditions, working late . . .'

In a similar case described by Vroom the manager decided to allow the team to develop by asking them to solve the problem themselves – GII. After having to be convinced that the manager meant it, they came up with the suggestion that the manager should have one reserved parking space and the rest would *all* use the public car park. The manager disagreed that he should have special privileges and it was agreed that everyone would use the public car park. Several years on, when all the team had moved on, the office still used the public car park and the special places were still used for customers and visitors.

In the second case of the research laboratory some of the same issues occur. The manager does not share the same goals as the team and although he could make a decision unaided, it is unlikely that such a decision would really work. There is a new element which we will term **quality of decision**. It is as if someone outside is watching over the decision and actually judging it – any decision will not do, the correct decision matters and a logical decision, given time, is probably possible. Looking at the process without any of the rules we will discuss later, we might see ourselves in either CI or CII.

Consider CI first.

MANAGER

SUBORDINATE A   SUBORDINATE B   SUBORDINATE C . . .

The manager has to act as a filter to the information coming from the subordinates and just as in our earlier issue of the Bank Manager, he or she does not really have the data to know who is lobbying from a genuine position. He or she would feel all the time that *they* are either getting together behind closed doors or that there was a paranoid atmosphere being built up where trust was vanishing behind the door. A CII would be an experience that few managers would wish to confront and one could well imagine entrenched positions becoming more entrenched and one's own leadership irrevocably challenged in public. Many managers given the choice have come up with a mixed style – AII with a few 'supporters' allowing the complexity of the problem to be spread in the team, followed by vigorous lobbying in CI. The climax would be a CII after the manager had checked out on alternative employment prospects. Nobody ever said management was going to be easy. In the Vroom parallel case the manager used AI with missiles – he wrote a letter announcing his decision and took the day off. The first members of the team left in about three months and the laboratory was closed in two years.

In the last case – the automation problem – the manager has no expert knowledge, no hard data but the team does share the problem and will probably go with any solution proposed. The manager concerned in a very similar case tried a form of GII:

'Look I need your help and I have to have it for 12.00. Come to some form of consensus on what we have to do and I will present it to senior management. If you have nothing by the meeting I will simply toss a coin and good luck to all of us.'

He did not get a decision by 12.00 and made his threat of a guess again, this time increasing the time limit to 12.30. At 12.30 he was presented with a compromise potential answer which he presented to the board. The compromise had the seeds of the full solution which was in turn implemented.

In going through the five cases, including those of the banker and Erickson, the captain at war, certain issues have recurred in defining the situation surrounding the choice of management decision-making styles.

A. *The Quality of the Decision*

The question is whether we need a decision or whether we need the correct decision against some externally imposed criteria. The captain and the manager with the car-parking problem needed to take action and virtually anything would have been accepted by people not directly concerned. In the other three cases someone else is watching, or will be watching if we get it wrong. Examples of decisions with a quality requirement would involve time, money, resources, legal implications and less easily defined factors concerned with image, precedent and correctness.

B. *Information*

Do you as the decision-maker, have enough data or expertise to make the decision unaided?

This time we are discussing information relating directly to the technical aspects of the decision, not the information that would make its acceptance more 'comfortable' to others.

The captain, and the operations manager did not have enough information whereas the research manager and office manager with the car problem arguably did.

C. *Logical Structure*

Do you as the manager, either by experience or analysis, understand what needs to be done and what data need to be collected for a high-quality decision? Do you know how to collect the alternatives and the rules that govern their selection?

If the problem has a logical structure we can almost think about it in the form of a matrix – cells of which need to be filled to collect the prize.

The research manager had a structured problem and the bank manager decided that the problem needed to be forced into a harsh structure to be solved.

D. *Acceptance*

Do we as the decision-maker need the commitment of others to get the decision implemented? Do others care strongly enough about the result of the decision to block or sabotage certain courses of action if they do not agree? Would monitoring of certain decisions be a problem?

We are talking about situations where others have to execute the decision using initiative, judgement, concern or, at minimum, compliance, and where supervision is likely to be at a low level. We are considering cases where others could feel strongly and where any resistance to the decision, whether active or passive, overt or covert, could block effective implementation.

The captain had it made for acceptance as did the operations manager but the car-parking manager did not. The R&D manager had needed even greater acceptance by the team and ignoring these had in practice closed the laboratory.

E. *Power*

We have already discussed the sources of power which give the decision-maker more latitude. I like to think of power as potential energy – power accepted is power held but power used is power lost. If you have to use raw power in your management job to get things done, your power will become exhausted.

F. *Shared Goals*

Do your subordinates share the same goals as you, the decision-maker?

We are asking whether the objectives of the decision-making process, as perceived by you, acting hopefully for the organisation or group as a whole, are the same as those of the group or the individuals in the group. For instance, in the case of the R&D manager the whole group probably wants to preserve its academic status and individuals their own projects, both these needs being independent of the needs of the organisation for immediate improved cash-flow through the exploitation of their technologies.

G. *Conflict within the Group*

Even if the group may share the overall goals of the organisation, certain potential solutions may be liable to cause conflict within the group. Thus in the car-parking case study the organisational goals are likely to be shared between the manager and the group but individuals will feel that certain potential solutions give unfair favours to others in the group – 'The Marketing Director has a space and here I am in production having to use the public car park.'

H. *Time Limits*

Time is a factor that bears on all decision-makers, the tighter the time pressures the greater the pressure for the decisions without consultation. Consultation involves others, trains others and promotes a team spirit but it takes time.

So we have eight questions when considering the form of management decision-making.

The Quality of the Decision
Can a good decision be judged against a bad one?

Information avaliable
Is enough information available for a quality decision?

Structure or Logic
Given time, can everything be worked out logically?

Acceptance
Does it matter if others do not agree?

Personal Power of the Decision-maker
Does the decision-maker have sufficient power to act alone?

Shared Goals or Objectives
Do the others share the same goals?

Conflict in the Group
Are the others split over some possible solutions?

Time Constraints
Are there overriding time constraints?

Using these eight questions in order, Vroom and his followers have been able to structure the management decision-making process. The model they use works in the following way – we work along the questions giving Yes or No. Let's look first at the problem of the bank manager.

A.   Yes – there is a quality requirement in that the head office, if not to say the police, are looking over the manager's shoulders. We move to the second question on information.

B.   Yes, we do have enough information to make a quality decision – if we look clearly at the problem, we do know that there have been irregularities and we do not need to understand their exact cause. If we decide to investigate and do not accept our mission – 'to get the branch back on course', we could well find ourselves going on the wrong track. We move directly to D.

D.   No – the acceptance of the subordinates, regardless of our feelings, is not necessary for effective implementation . . . AI.

Decision Model

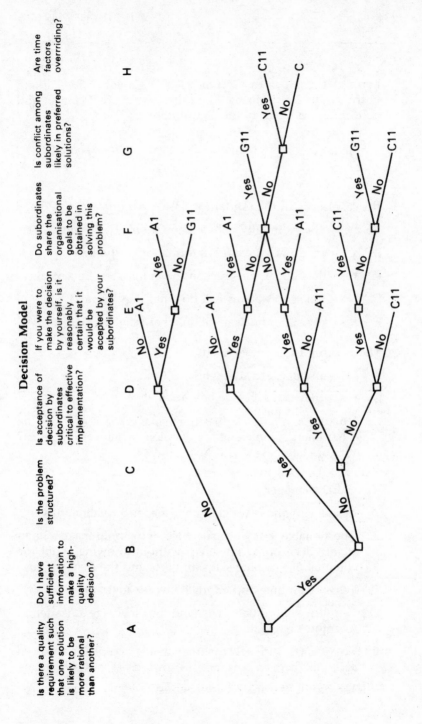

A	B	C	D	E	F	G	H
Is there a quality requirement such that one solution is likely to be more rational than another?	Do I have sufficient information to make a high-quality decision?	Is the problem structured?	Is acceptance of decision by subordinates critical to effective implementation?	If you were to make the decision by yourself, is it reasonably certain that it would be accepted by your subordinates?	Do subordinates share the organisational goals to be obtained in solving this problem?	Is conflict among subordinates likely in preferred solutions?	Are time factors overrriding?

EXERCISE

Look at the other case studies – the Captain, the Parking Problem, the R&D Manager and the Operations Manager and go through the logic of the algorithm.

The case study of **the Captain** yields to AII thus:

A   Yes – the Admiralty will demand a quality decision.

B   No – we do not have full information at the time.

C   Yes – the Captain's instructions cover this sort of eventuality.

D   No – the subordinates will do what they are told.

E   Yes – the subordinates will do what they are told . . . AII.

The Parking Problem yields thus:

A   No – any decision that works is OK.

D   Yes – they can sabotage any decision.

E   A matter of opinion – does the manager want to waste his or her energy in making the decision, whatever it is, stick? If he or she does – AI, if not, GII.

The R&D Manager

A   Yes – everyone is watching and needs a quality answer.

B   Questionable, but we suspect No, we cannot make a high-quality decision by ourselves without knowing about the potential of the 'blue skies' projects and their champions.

C   Yes – given time and effort, there is a logical basis.

D   Yes – the subordinates will (and did) sabotage any attempt to enforce a decision.

E   No – it is very unlikely that they would accept any enforced decision. There really is pressure towards a C or G resolution.

If we decide the answer to B is Yes:

F   No – they have completely different roles.

G   Questionable – they might agree to oppose everything so we have CI and lobbying or they might be split and CII.

(Question B reaches the same set if we answer Yes)

The Operational Manager

A   No – we need something to try.

D   Questionable as is E, so we have either AI or GII, depending on your opinion of your authority. With the extra dimension of time constraints most managers would choose AI but the manager concerned chose GII with an imposed AI.

GII has a problem with numbers and the normal accepted figure is that GII without help does not work when more than seven are involved. However, 'with help' much larger numbers can be involved.

> We were called upon by an importer of cars from the Eastern Bloc to run a GII meeting for all middle managers. The venue of the meeting was chosen as an isolated hotel over a weekend and the meeting started with the Managing Director giving very stark news of the balance sheet. In the last year the company had lost half its business and was heading for bankruptcy. A plan for survival was needed. The MD then announced that he was leaving and would return on Sunday afternoon to endorse the plan developed by the group of his managers, and he left. We ran a brainstorming session for ideas and at 200, we stopped and separated the ideas into the company functions – marketing, manufacture, distribution, accounts . . . At the hour, on the hour, each of the groups reported to plenary and went away again to refine their ideas.
>
> When the MD returned, the managers had come up with a drastic reorganisation, well beyond the scope of anything he could have suggested without consent.

————————▶

EXERCISE

Look back at your own management decision-making process and go through the logic of the algorithm.

Does the analysis fit your preferred process?

Are there any problems in answering the questions?

Look at the issues that arise from the problems – are they because of your own lack of understanding of the way people will react to you or are they due to lack of clarity in your purpose?

⎯⎯⎯⎯▶

The algorithm is intended to show how the choice of decision-making method can be structured but is not intended to *tell* you how to proceed. We do not expect you to stick a copy on the wall and ask your subordinates to wait while you consult the oracle. We do ask you to consider that alternatives do exist to your pressurised behaviour and that allowing the Adult to direct your choice may well save you a number of problems.

In the next chapter we will look at all the issues that Aware Managers need to have in their heads while making choices and in particular when making choices related to change.

CHAPTER EIGHT

The Manager as a Juggler

'There are so many things to think of and nothing stays still.'

'Managing is like picking up wet soap – get it right for a second and it slips out of your hand again.'

In the last chapters we discussed the Aware Manager both as an individual and as somebody who has to deal with others, some of whom do not share the same goals. We are now going to look at the job of the manager in its entirety and not just from the aspect of dealing with people. The point we are going to make is that a good manager is like an immensely skilled juggler who has to keep a number of plates spinning simultaneously. The analogy is not quite complex enough, however, since for the manager all the plates seem to be connected and any change in any one of the plates affects the properties of the rest. Good managers, be they executive or advisory, have to be very skilled jugglers indeed because the plates have to be made to spin simultaneously on a table that is far from steady. We have already discussed the way in which we steer our *style* of management towards using our valued skills. Here we are going to discuss how we also steer the actual content of what we manage towards using our valued skills. Returning to our analogy of the juggler – all of us are likely to have favourite plates – certain valued parts of the job that we find satisfying, and while we concentrate our efforts on these valued plates, other plates may well lose momentum and fall to the ground.

In discussing the role of manager we will be discussing one of the most difficult jobs we are ever likely to be asked to perform – charting our way through change.

However:
No chart is of any use unless you know your present position.

THE FIVE SPINNING PLATES OF THE AWARE MANAGER

The Management job can be seen as having five elements:

> Maintaining objectives – PURPOSE
> Facilitating, controlling and leading people – TEAM
> Establishing and maintaining morale – REWARDS
> Developing and monitoring
> an appropriate organisation – STRUCTURES
> Fostering and liaising
> for a helpful climate – FAIR WINDS
>
> How each element is handled depends on the manager,
> the staff and the circumstance.

In our analogy we see each of the five elements as plates that need to be kept spinning.

The Plate labelled PURPOSE

There is no specific order implied in our discussion of the plates since they all interact with each other – changes to one plate may well affect each and every other plate. However, we have to start somewhere and the first plate we will discuss is labelled – PURPOSE.

'If you don't know where you are going you will finish up somewhere else'

is an aphorism we have used before. The Aware Manager needs to understand what is required of him or her as a significant part of understanding the starting position.

———▶

EXERCISE

Attempt to answer the following questions about your job.

(a) What business are we in, what is our aim?
(b) How am I judged and how is my group judged, and by whom?
(c) Is the purpose coherent and specific?

and   (d)   If I cannot answer any of the previous three questions – How do I find out the answers?

⟶

It is perfectly possible to tread water in a management job without establishing exactly what your purpose is, but treading water over an extended period, as many of us know, is a dangerous and unrewarding pastime.

Anyone will be able to tell you your naive Purpose for a particular job, but the ready definition is inclined to be less than helpful. Establishing the real Purpose can take a great deal of effort and in the case of whole organisations, can take years.

Imagine you are in charge of the analytical department of a paints company. The naive purpose as developed by your group could be 'to analyse incoming raw materials and check the quality of the company products against specification'. Accepting this definition the manager might well find him or herself in continuous battles with production, who might have their purpose defined as 'getting the maximum amount of product through the door at minimum cost and acceptable quality'. An actual and acceptable purpose of your analytical group might well be defined effectively as for instance:

To understand the issues of production so that no raw materials will be allowed to pass without the necessity of any further processing and hence problems with the production process.

To provide data to the purchasing department so that more favourable contracts can be made with suppliers.

To redefine the product specification in terms of why the customer chooses the company's product against the competition.

To assist a 'right first time' system in production so that no rejects are necessary.

Any manager accepting the original naive purpose and who strove for professional excellence through achieving it, could well alienate him or herself from the rest of the organisation. The naive Purpose is an isolated judgemental one whereas the actual revised and developed Purpose is concerned with liaison. The Aware Manager in any job needs to be conscious all the time that the Purpose of his or her function can change with every breeze on the organisation. An example could well be for the chemical analyst in our example who might find that the market has hardened and that his organisation's world has become dominated by over-capacity. The new Purpose of the analytical group could now well be concerned with rejecting batches of raw materials and product so that production can adjust its capacity more cheaply.

The Purpose of a group need not necessarily be an active one. The purpose may be to 'be available', 'look good on the company report' or indeed be the 'poison pill' for hostile predators. The Aware Manager needs to be very clear and understand his or her ambitions against what is required to keep the 'Plate labelled Purpose' spinning. However, while we correctly concern ourselves with Purpose, we need to keep the other plates serviced and spinning. For instance without people, the manager has no tools. Thus we move to the next plate.

The Plate labelled TEAM

Observations on my reading history, in Library, May Nineteen, Seventeen Hundred Thirty-one:

That the great affairs of this world, the wars, revolutions, etc., are carried on and effected by parties.

That the view of these parties is their present general interest, or what they take to be such.

That the different views of these different parties occasion all confusion.

That while a party is carrying on a general design, each man has his particular private interest in view.

That as soon as a party has gained its general point, each member becomes intent upon his particular interest; which, thwarting others, breaks that party into divisions, and occasions more confusion.

– Benjamin Franklin as quoted by Eric Berne.

Franklin, in 1731, was saying what all Aware Managers must have worked out for themselves: to achieve anything effectively you need a team with a clear purpose. Without that purpose, or when that purpose is achieved, individual issues and the issues of individuals will destroy the team – if you let it happen.

So how do we keep the 'Plate labelled Team' spinning?

Firstly, the manager needs to be concerned with keeping the team in touch with the purpose. 'Keeping the team in touch with the purpose' will include supplying the facilities, the controls and the direction the team needs to fulfil that purpose – a great deal of work in the Questioning quadrant. Should, however, the purpose be weak or unclear the manager needs to be able to take firmer control of the individuals and the group – the management style will have to move away from consensus GII and Consultative CI/CII to AI/AII – the Practical Manager approach. Secondly and again working from the Questioning quadrant, the manager needs to understand the relevant needs of individuals in the group. We are *not* asking the manager to become a universal social worker but to consider and put priority onto what is relevant.

> In the final Scott expedition to Antarctica it was relevant that Evans was undernourished and had lost essential strength. Evans was a larger man than the others and needed more than basic rations to survive. Scott by listening to his own mind music – the machismo Be Strong theme – while dealing with Evans and not allowing any special pleading probably contributed to Evans' death and the failure of the whole expedition. The Practical Manager approach was not the most effective.
>
> The Aware Manager listens to individuals and reserves the time to understand what may be relevant.

Thirdly, the manager needs to understand the needs of the group in relation to the Purpose, the facilities and the individuals within it – this could well be familiar ground for the Resource Managers among our readers but they, too, need to find out what are the 'needs of the group'. They may also question the distinction we made between 'group' and 'team'. The difference between a 'team' and a 'group' is crucial and in discussing it many of the issues concerning the management of the Plate called Team will emerge.

> A team is a group of people dedicated towards a goal – a purpose. Every team is a group but only the rare group is a team.

The process of movement from group to team is in four stages:

STAGE 1 – JOINING AND BELONGING

At first we have a basic group of people who have been brought together and are unclear of the reasons for their presence – both as a group and as individuals. The group may stay in this undeveloped stage indefinitely if:

(a)   The task remains unclear;
(b)   There is genuine or perceived insecurity of group membership;
(c)   The management decision-making style remains in AI and the group depends on external decisions for its purpose and patterns to be decided.

The group will return to the undeveloped stage should any of these factors return – the task changes, redundancy threatens, people leave or join. An Aware Manager working in an authoritarian management structure or with a task which is changing uncontrollably, may well choose to keep the team in the undeveloped Joining and Belonging stage.

STAGE 2 – ROLE AND CONTROL

Here we have a group which has established some definition of its task and understands that all its members are required to be present but it is not exactly clear what roles everyone has to perform. The formal leadership is probably accepted but the informal pecking orders are not. Consultation is possible but it is always consultation marred by suspicion – 'I'm not certain why the boss is asking her, she only graduated last year . . .' The group may stay in this rather uncomfortable developing stage if:

(a)   The task or tasks have hidden agenda, e.g. among graduate trainees the spoken task may be to complete a particular job on target but the hidden agenda is to be noticed by senior management for future promotion.
(b)   The roles demanded by functions do not fit the preferred way individuals wish to work. Thus we may have more than one person in the group who has 'valued skills' in the same area, say in controlling others. It could well be in these circumstances that the battle for supremacy in the group could extend until the group disbands in acrimony.
(c)   The management decision-making style remains predominantly authoritarian or consultative with no experiments in consensus – GII to allow it to form its own informal structures.

The Aware Manager who has a task requiring competition for success – a high-pressure sales team – may well choose to keep the team in the Role and Control Stage.

STAGE 3 – PAIRING AND SHARING

Here the group can be seen by the outsider as becoming a team. The individuals in the group/team no longer need to jockey for position and are valued as members of something that can be given a discrete title – be it the 'Boffins' or 'Accounts'. People are in the process of finding out who they like to work with and who they can trust on an intimate level.

The process of moving from the second stage of the Role and Control battles to the maturing of the Pairing and Sharing stage will most probably have involved some individuals deciding that they are *not* wanted or that they do not accept the roles upon which the success of the team depends. In this case they will choose their moment and leave.

A mutual enemy may well have been found for this stage of group/team development and this 'mutual enemy' may well *be* the manager, and even if it is not, may well give the manager a problem.

> An organisation hired a non-trainer to take over its training centre and replace its existing and popular manager. The centre, geo-graphically separated from the rest of the organisation seemed to be functioning efficiently and the visitors met an almost benign atmosphere as they came through the doors. All the staff functioned well together but perhaps a little too well. The new manager after he had recovered from the surprise of his appointment was granted an interview with a senior member of the head office personnel:
>
> 'Basically your job is to break the group up. They have become alienated from the organisation and seem to be working for them-selves.'
>
> The enemy that had united the group and made it a Stage 3 team, was the paymaster – the organisation itself.

The team/group may well stay in Stage 3 if:

(a) The group is allowed to modify the task to suit its 'valued skills' without monitoring.

(b) The fit of personality is 'too good'; and there is no 'sand in the oyster to produce the pearl'.

(c) The team membership is static.

(d) The management decision-making style has become the consensus GII *as of right*.

An Aware Manager who understands that his or her team is likely to be needed in the future for a not yet defined Purpose, may well allow the team to remain as a consolidating team in the Pairing and Sharing stage and avoid some of the issues of the Mature Team.

STAGE 4 – THE MATURE TEAM

The mature team is a team of professionals who take personal and collective responsibility for their actions:

> 'I am sorry but Pat is out of the office at the moment. I can see from her notes that she would want you to buy the steelwork at that price for delivery but obviously I cannot give you complete authority. Put in a provisional order and I will get Pat to ring back. Yes, Henry Patterson, Patterson with two t's.'

Living in a Mature Team is an experience which rarely lasts for long and should be savoured, as any European Association Football manager would agree.

The Mature Team will survive if:

(a)   The task and the membership have evolved together.
(b)   The management adopts a situational style of decision making from AI/AII to GII as appropriate.
(c)   Outside factors allow it.

The Fly on the Wall will notice:

For a Stage 1 Undeveloped Team working on Joining and Belonging issues –

Grumbling on immediate conditions.
Intellectualising.
Swift 'dashes' to complete tasks.
One-sided definitions of position.
Temporary and stereotyped groupings.
Suspicion and time spent on attributing blame.
Total reliance on *them* or the boss.

For a Stage 2 Developing Team working on Role and control issues –

Defensiveness, competition and jealousy.
Challenges to Structure and task.
Experimental hostility and aggro.
Ambivalence to the appointed leader.
'Stag fights' and 'try-ons'.
Intense brittle links and cliques.

Tantrums or impatience from individuals who *know* their skills match the task.

For a Stage 3 consolidating Team working on Pairing and Sharing issues –

Potential alienation from other teams.
Blossoming of private relationships.
Redefinition of physical boundaries.
Lack of formal leadership control.

$$\longrightarrow$$

EXERCISE

From what you have read of the stages of team development, here and elsewhere, in what stage would you put your own home team?

(a)   Is this stage of development sensible and appropriate for the task of the team?
(b)   If it is not, what can and should I do to change the situation?

$$\longrightarrow$$

There is no pressure from the author to persuade a manager that the Mature Team is the only or indeed best tool for working. The Mature Team is a beautifully honed machine that will excel in the clear and defined tasks it is given – however, the Mature Team *needs* to be kept busy or it finds something else to do. If for the multitude of reasons that the real world provides, there are not enough clear and defined tasks, then the mature team will find them, and that is not always what is wanted.

A mature team had developed during the first few days of a training programme at a management centre. The task given to the team was to build a replica tower of children's building bricks from an example in another room. One member of the team had been dispatched to the other room to relay the design. Unfortunately the member sent to relay the design was a very precise individual who took an inordinate time with structural drawings.

When finally the drawings were perfect the messenger returned to the team to find that they had 'completed' the task and built a rather stylish tower to their own satisfaction and own design. The team also resented any form of criticism that they had not done very well.

Managers of all but the Undeveloped Team will find themselves in the potentially uncomfortable position of serving as well as controlling the team. It is this, the paradox of manager as facilitator/servant against manager as boss, that defeats many budding Aware Managers. It is a lot more comfortable for many managers to remain in their own preferred quadrant – Facilitator, Resource Controller, Practical or Action. Any developing team *demands* situational management or it regresses, either on its own or with outside pressures, to being an undeveloped team.

Being part of a team – belonging, fitting into a human hierarchy and working with personally respected individuals brings its own **rewards**.

The Plate labelled REWARDS

The term Rewards covers the whole issue of 'Why do we do the job?' and is as complex as the individuals and groups with which we work. We may give work for money, vengeance, to establish order, to be allowed to give orders, to help others, to belong . . . or any combination of these. The list and combinations are virtually endless, but using the language of this book, can be made very simple:

We derive personal satisfaction at work by:

Using our skills effectively towards our respected goals

Working with others – belonging in a team
– having a position in a team
– relating to specific individuals.

The level of 'personal satisfaction' needed, varies from individual to individual, as does the split between the Job and the People factors.

The inventory below is reprinted from *The New Manager* and designed to allow the reader to determine what we have called 'the split between Job and People factors.'

Working style inventory

Give a total of ten marks to each set of questions, allocated as you see fit. Thus Question 1 could be (a) 3, (b) 0, (c) 2, (d) 5 = total 10.

Question 1
When you arrive at the office, do you:
- (a) want to get straight down to work?
- (b) find out what everyone has been doing the previous day?
- (c) check up whether your instructions have been carried out?
- (d) have an informal chat with a lieutenant?

Question 2
When you are invited to a firm's party, do you:
- (a) think it's part of the job, but hope you are overseas at the time?
- (b) look forward to it?
- (c) remember you are organising it anyway?
- (d) look forward to meeting some old mates?

Question 3
When you start working in a large group, do you:
- (a) get into a corner and start work while they argue?
- (b) worry whether you actually belong?
- (c) get down to restoring order from the people chaos, or try to find out what role you are to play?
- (d) look round for friendly faces?

Question 4
When you have to work away from base, do you:
- (a) hope that they follow your clear instructions?
- (b) feel that you may be left out of it on return?
- (c) make regular checks to see that they are on course?
- (d) delegate to a lieutenant and exchange phone calls?

Question 5
If invited to present your work to a conference, do you:
- (a) concentrate on the written presentation?
- (b) get most concerned with the oral presentation?
- (c) get involved with the organisation?
- (d) look forward to the discussions after formal work?

The totals should add up to 50.
Your (a) total is _____
Your (b) total is _____
    (c) total is _____
    (d) total is _____   Total of (b) + (c) + (d) _____

The (a) score relates to our attention to task and out of a total of 50 points anyone with over 20 in (a) is very task orientated; (b), (c) and (d) are related to the Joining and Belonging, Role and Control, and Pairing and Sharing needs respectively.

We have already discussed using our 'valued skills' but we may have skated too quickly over our 'respected goals'. In the chapter where we discussed 'sector people' we mentioned that individual parts of the problem-solving process involved using sets of valued skills and that *given a choice* many managers would specialise in working on one or more areas. Thus we had the Facilitator Manager working from the Questioning quadrant, who saw management in terms of allowing and helping others to work effectively – our example was Henry Hamid. Similarly we had Dennis our Resource Manager who worked from the Logical quadrant, Campbell our Practical Manager and Betty our Action Manager. The goals each of our four would be seeking would differ widely. Henry would be proud of the success of 'his' people and the way they were developing. Dennis would derive great satisfaction from his skilled structuring of his section and the accuracy of its work. Campbell, our Practical Manager would pride himself on the professionalism of his work and Betty would look for *results*.

————————▶

EXERCISE

Look back at your own view of your valued skills as a manager and the rough distribution of your energy into the quadrants.

Think of your own valued incidents and see them in terms of the rewards you get from the job. List these rewards.

————————▶

The second set of issues concerned with rewards is concerned with Team membership. We have said that each of us personally needs other people to a greater or lesser extent and that this need can be conveniently split into a classification parallel to the stages of team development. We may have high Joining and Belonging needs and not slip easily into groups – we need to be made welcome and when we are made welcome we work more effectively. Others, the Travelling Salespersons of the world, can bob in and out of groups as the task dictates. We may have a high need for knowing our status in a group – we have high Role and Control needs. If we do have high Role and Control needs we look for job clarity and will work for it. We prefer clear job specifications, and vague instructions will annoy us. People with high Pairing and Sharing needs are happy having a small set of intimates they can trust. It is perfectly possible to have needs in all the three classifications but many of us have particular people needs, and attempt to adjust our jobs accordingly to achieve our balance of people rewards from the teams we are attached to. Looking at Henry's downfall with the process worker in this light we might conclude that he had high Pairing and Sharing needs and this is one perspective on why he was grateful to the man for admitting his fault and not forcing Henry to alienate him by discipline. Each and every team we belong to provides some of the personal satisfactions that we derive from working with other people. Our needs for working satisfaction are derived in doing a job we value *and* in working with others – the balance of our need for working with others being distributed between people *en masse* – our Joining and Belonging needs, our need for clarity and control – our Role and Control needs and our need for individual human contact – our Pairing and Sharing needs. All of us belong to other teams, and all of these teams may enter into the personal satisfaction equation and it would be surprising if all the teams and sub-teams to which we belong were in the same state of development and offered the same rewards for member-ship. The changes each of the teams undergoes often have subtle effects on the rewards you and your subordinates derive from their membership, and these changes need to be reviewed over time. Think for instance, of a successful salesman who is pro-moted to a desk job – the sub-team that might well have given him or her most rewards is likely to include customers, and working from a desk this whole set of personal satisfactions is lost. Unless the job compensates, the promoted salesman will be unsatisfied and will have to find new relationships. A major prob-lem you may have as an Aware Manager is the membership of your own team and of the 'management team'. You will be called upon in two roles – as representative of your own constituency and as a loyal supporter of the management team.

———————▶

EXERCISE

In your working team:

(a)   How is good work rewarded?
(b)   How is work appraised?
(c)   Are there some high and some low profile jobs around?
(d)   What is the norm of the team – is it for good work or is it for 'getting by'?
(e)   Who gives the rewards?
(f)   Is the reward 'system', such as it is, appropriate to the staff involved?
(g)   How do you give and receive rewards yourself?
(h)   What rewards do individuals get from being in *your* team and is is likely that on balance it is for the various sub-teams to which you and they belong to provide the major rewards for the job – customers, unions, sports and social clubs . . .?

———————▶

When we get down to looking at some case studies we will see just how the reward system may well be the first plate to fall when change is imposed.

Our next plate belòngs to the organisation, and indeed *is* the organisation.

The Plate labelled STRUCTURES

'When in doubt – reorganise.'

The whole decade of the 1970s seemed to be devoted to bigger and better structures. The slightest problem in an organisation would be greeted by a memorandum announcing the latest

WORKING IN TEAMS

We derive our personal satisfaction at work in two ways:
Using our valued skills
Working with people

We all work in several teams

The team giving us most personal satisfaction gains our
greatest loyalty

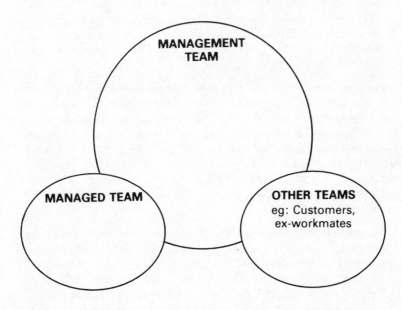

We all need other people to satisfy:
- our Joining and Belonging needs

- our Role and Control needs

- our Pairing and Sharing needs

We differ:
- in how MUCH we need others
- our distribution of needs between J&B, R&C and P&S
- where we get our needs met

reorganisation, and often the organisational charts were out of date before they had appeared on the noticeboards. For a short period the formal organisation charts were even circulated with 'influence diagrams' and then, quite suddenly with real pressures to get things working more effectively, reorganisation seemed to be done in a less public manner; but times may change again.

An effective structure is about an appropriate division of work. It may also be about the public recognition of responsibility but essentially it is about doing the task more efficiently, informing new members of the group on procedures, managing conflicts before they arise and providing a formula for sharing rewards.

> An example of an ideal 'structure' could be the school timetable. By looking at the school timetable you can tell who is supposed to be where, when, and teaching who, what. Informally Mr X may ask Ms Y to take French in 5G, but it is formally accepted that Mr X is responsible. The timetable also shows publicly how duties and responsibilities are being allocated.

R&D teams are notoriously difficult to organise and for years the job was seen as impossible – 'creativity might be stifled'. The over-organisation of R&D as typified by the Rothschild Report in the UK had the effect of making scientists and technicians conscious of commercial motives but perhaps too conscious and the reins were slackened again. A new, more intelligent view of the system for the organisation of R&D is appearing.

Connell in 1985 was asked to advise on the structure of hi-tech companies:

> The key to the success of hi-tech companies is their ability to convert new technological development into commercial products or services. And it is the creativity of the company's scientists that underpins this process. At the same time, the development process itself must be very well managed if new products are to be brought to market within budget and ahead of competitors.
>
> Good products management is absolutely essential in R&D based companies, but it is especially important in hard companies. Without this discipline, overruns can easily occur, and products may be over-engineered as scientists struggle to achieve a degree of perfection which is not commercially justified. Product management involves six key elements:
>
> (a) Clear technical and cost specifications, based on the overall;

(b)   Detailed planning of the tasks involved and the resources to be used in undertaking them (i.e. people, finance, equipment);

(c)   Organising those resources in a way which enables them to be co-ordinated effectively;

(d)   Milestones, with clear outputs, against which progress can be checked at intervals during the development programme;

(e)   Disciplined and regular progress monitoring with regular re-estimating of the time of completion;

(f)   Formal mechanisms for authorising change to the product specifications or the development effort planned.

Some degree of creative licence of the company's scientists is essential to foster this process. However, it is important to control it within clear guidelines, so that the amount of time spent on longer-term development work is kept in check, R&D is focused on the strategic objectives of the business, and priority projects are completed as quickly and effectively as possible.

The mechanisms that would allow Connell's ideal to be fulfilled would certainly involve attaching great importance to a 'Plate labelled Structure' while of course keeping an eye on all the other plates.

$\longrightarrow$

EXERCISE

Look at your own job and answer the following questions on Structure:

(a)   How would you define the structure of your group/team?

(b)   Do you have clear systems and procedures?

(c)   Who benefits from the systems, procedures and general structure?

(d)   Is the structure appropriate now?

(e)   Is the structure understood, adhered to and accepted?

$\longrightarrow$

Whatever we decide on the first four plates, no group/team can exist in a vacuum and without some occasional outside support. And so we come to the final plate.

The Plate labelled FAIR WINDS

Fair Winds are the possibly accidental factors that make the management job easier. The Fair Winds may be contacts that have survived over many years and still have value now. They may be company procedures that allow one's own group that little extra latitude when things are hard. The Fair Winds may well escape your notice because they 'just happen to be there' but they need fostering – a process of continuous maintenance for your job to succeed. At the minimum, Fair Winds need to be recognised and understood.

> Clarke Built, an industrial refrigerator manufacturer, moved from their shabby East London factory to a modern purpose-designed plant in a new town. Once there, they realised one 'fair wind' they had lost. In the East London plant they were able to call upon skilled jobbing machinists at virtually any time of day or night for unscheduled repair work. No such facility existed in the new town and it cost them a lot of money to develop their own.

Finding one's own Fair Winds is often difficult since they may only be known to a very restricted group in the whole organisation, and it may be in their immediate interest to keep the information from 'management'.

———————▶

EXERCISE

Look at your own job

(a) What Fair Winds do you count on?
(b) How important are they and how vulnerable are they?
(c) Do you devote enough time to the liaison function so that you understand and foster your Fair Winds?

———————▶

Using the analogy of the five spinning plates, we can now review the appropriateness of our approach to management.

There are managers who are themselves in a continuous fire-fighting role – as perhaps was Betty – dashing round the table holding the plates giving each of them a twist to keep them all in motion. We can imagine favourite plates that seem to respond to our special twist and give us great pleasure, and plates which always seem to be falling off the table and which basically annoy us. Campbell might well miss on allowing his 'plate called Team' to develop and devote too much attention to polishing his 'plate called Systems'. He might even allow the other plates to look after themselves, but all of us know that the process of 'looking after themselves' cannot be guaranteed at any time and certainly not in periods of change. We may have great admiration for the Aware Manager who seems to be able to spin the plates effortlessly on the ends of sticks and away from the table, while we are too busy stopping our own plates from wobbling off the table to even consider another and better way. The New Manager probably has an excuse for having to handle each of the plates but the professional Aware Manager knows that the sticks – planning, delegation, influence – are a more effective way of survival and growth.

What, however, happens when we have one of the plates exchanged, or altered in any way? What happens in change?

> The British Mental Health Service was developed from the set of Victorian values that considered that the very process of putting mentally sick people into grand buildings and allowing them institutional care, would help them towards a cure. From these values came a number of magnificent institutions with great rolling grounds ultimately paid for by the National Health Service and containing large numbers of long-term inmates. It was recognised in the 1980s that the inmates were not being 'cured' but that they were being institutionalised and it was decided to introduce a system of Community Care. The large institutions were to be phased out and patients put into small units dispersed throughout the community.

The system we are advocating for looking at change and predicting its consequences to you the Aware Manager consists of taking individual plates and seeing in detail how they are affected by the change. We then move onto other plates and see what the knock-on effects are – the implications of the changes from our first chosen plate to the others. When we have looked at all the plates, we consider the managerial issues of having to keep all the new, or revised plates, spinning. Virtually any plate can be the starting-point but we will, in this case, not begin with the most tendentious plate of the Mental Health case study – the 'Plate labelled Purpose' but start with the 'Plate labelled Team'.

The team from the Institution was a mature team, with very clear membership rules. It worked shifts and people had lockers and coffee mugs they owned and felt secure with. Individual relationships were strong both within the nursing staff and with the patients. The change meant that all this altered, and as one nursing sister put it:

'I used to have a place in front of a radiator and now I have a seat in a car behind a radiator – 'have Metro will travel'.

The team became fragmented and individual relations with the patients changed drastically.

Let's move onto the 'Plate labelled Rewards'. Everyone had, or felt they had, been there a long time. The Joining and Belonging, the Role and Control and Pairing and Sharing needs had all stabilised for all the team and the job had been adjusted so that their particular needs were met.

What were the rewards of the old job? Well, they were certainly connected with the Institution and institutionalisation. Problems were shared, and everyone knew everyone else, including the patients.

'I really looked forward to some of the birthdays – not a lot really, but special, and you need something special in this job.'

Who would give the birthday parties, such as they were, for the patients in the new system – the controllers of the Community Care Homes? The medical staff had become peripatetic administrators and controllers. The conversation in staff meetings was not the success of particular patients but problems with particular Care Homes. The cosy atmosphere had gone, hopefully to be replaced by a new professionalism – which should, in time, produce new rewards. The Fair Winds plate had changed as well. The whole mechanism of voluntary support at the Institution had gone and the issues with the community had changed as well. In the area of the Institution the locals knew what was happening and how to ignore or help. In the small units spread throughout the area new people met new challenges and complained every so often about the fall in house prices when the residential Care Centres were set up. It can take a long time for the Fair Winds to reform.

The structural changes were on two levels. Firstly, the move from the administration of large community-owned Victorian mansions to a number of small and mostly privately owned houses was considerable and obvious. Some areas of skills vanished altogether – the institutional catering unit for instance. The less obvious points came perhaps in the area of communications. In the old system it was possible to get all the staff together fairly rapidly in a central room and brief people on what was happening in virtually any style – GII to AI. The time constraints were understood and for many purposes the same for the whole staff. Now individuals worked to outside constraints and often to outside supervision.

Naively the 'Plate labelled Purpose' could be considered to be the same. We could think of the overall purpose of the Mental Health Care Service to be curing patients so that they could lead a healthy life in the community, but the world is more complicated. It is somehow concerned with the understanding that the patients and the community are not to be allowed to take the easy way out and isolate themselves from each other. Exactly how you would define the new purpose is less relevant than the overall consequences of the change. The old purpose allowed internal auditing, the new purpose was high profile.

What does this say about the change that you, as the Aware Manager controlling or advising within a part or all of the new organisation, would need to make in your way of keeping the plates spinning, your overall style of management?

The answer to our question depends very much on the style you have adopted previously. We could see you as an institutional administrator deriving a great deal of your rewards from knowing every part of the operation and being able to sense weaknesses and opportunities – the Resource Manager would thrive. We could, however, see you knowing many of your staff personally and at easy times, discussing cases as with equals and operating as a Facilitator Manager from the Questioning quadrant – if this was your preferred method of operation, then you would be much less happy. The new job would work well if you took on the role of an administrator and politician divorced from day-to-day contact with the staff, but perhaps your valued skills would not be used in this concept of management.

Before we ask you to look at a past or current change in your plate-spinning act, let's look at another case study.

———————▶

EXERCISE

In the early 1980s the major oil companies began to consider seriously that the science of palaeontology might be able to provide the tool to reduce the exploding cost of oil exploration. The palaeontologist using a microscope to look at fossils and the growing science of oil-bearing rocks, just could add to, if not substitute for, the information coming from seismic and other sources. Palaeontologists exist in three main branches – micropalaeontology, the study of small fossil creatures with hard skeletons, palaeobotany, the study of fossil plants, and palynology, the study of fossil spores and pollen. The highly skilled specialists were recruited from the universities. They had proved their worth in a few years and the oil companies' gambles had paid off.

Success was rewarded by a new brief to provide a service to their parent oil company exploration teams. The *purpose* is redefined:

Before – 'To establish whether the science of palaeontology can be used to assist the identification of oil-bearing strata and thus reduce the cost of exploration.'

After – 'To provide an effective and efficient palaeontology service to the world-wide oil exploration teams.'

How would you see other 'plates' changing and how would the 'ideal' management decision-making style need to change as well? How would you manage to keep all the plates on the table spinning during and after the change?

———————————————▶

Starting with the Plate labelled Structures. Originally the Structure was in the three sub-disciplines of palaeontology, each with strong roots in their old university departments. Their old supervisors were interested in the new work and able to offer advice and free consultancy – a great measure of what we have called Fair Winds. The new Structure needs to provide a total service and the customers – the oil exploration teams spread throughout the world – are hardly likely to want to deal with three different experts for any one question. The three sub-disciplines need to work in one team, each team responsible for an exploration area – North Sea, South America, China Sea . . .

For the Fair Winds – the university contacts – the changes were major, what had happened was that a science had become a technology. With this, and the inevitable cloak of commercial secrecy, many of the rewards arising out of sub-team member- ship had gone. The oil company palaeontologists were no longer welcome contributors to academic conferences and needed to pay for consultancy from their former colleagues.

We could continue the case analysis but perhaps we have said enough. The manager/palaeontologist will no longer be able to function with GII predominant as a first among equals but will be forced to adopt an appropriate organisational style moving between AI and GII as the situation arises with a major issue being the management style of the much larger team with which the group is now associated.

▶

EXERCISE

Look at a change that has occurred or is about to occur in your job and 'study the plates' before and after the change.

Use the methodology we have described taking one plate you consider key and see how it affects the other plates in turn. Finally look at your own predominant and preferred style of leadership before the change and consider dispassionately what the ideal style *should* be now. How do you shape up?

➡

Our next chapter will deal with the final question we posed ourselves – Was it *them*? We will attempt to show how you can adopt the dispassionate stance of an outsider to your organisation and see whether, with you in a position of responsibility, it will survive the unavoidable changes ahead. We will also attempt to extend your own ability to allow the organisation to survive and prosper in a world of complex change.

CHAPTER NINE

Success is the Time to Worry – The Ecology of Organisations

'I understand that the whole organisation needs to change to survive but the whole structure seems to be designed to resist change of any sort.'

'So we may be vulnerable – where do I start looking?'

'If I understood what made the whole business tick, I might have a chance.'

'It used to fit – really neat business – but now it seems out of step.'

'Is it me, or is it them and do I still want to play?'

We began this book by looking at the issues you, the reader had in working with your fellow human beings as you matured in your job. We then moved on to your role as an experienced manager and discussed the teams and groups with which you associate. In this chapter we are going to discuss **the organisation**, the shell that confines, but also permits your activities as a manager.

Organisations are designed to provide the inertia that makes work possible, but organisations must always live in the past. They are designed or evolved to fit a past set of circumstances, or at best a present or future set of circumstances viewed from the past. Strangely, the present perfection of an organisation is a clue to future problems.

The British store group Marks and Spencer recognised its 'perfection' in the late 1970s. In a way that frightened some of its managers it was ideally suited for the times and was immensely profitable. The problem for senior management was that 'times' were certainly going to change. How do you move from success?

A senior training manager of the high technology company Hewlett Packard described a problem he had in training. His company had been listed in the management classic *In Search of Excellence* as an example of quality in its area. How do you get managers to understand the need to change or indeed accept training in these circumstances?

The UK frozen food company Birds Eye at its 21st birthday was able to announce an annual growth of just less than 21 per cent. An inspired policy of buying, marketing and quality control had worked for that period. In the next year a combination of problems of supply and changes in retail patterns reduced its growth to a snail's pace.

In this chapter we are going to look initially at the factors that together make an organisation ideally suited to its environment at a particular point in its development and then we will move on to a method of reviewing the vulnerability of these factors to changes of any sort.

We are going to make the claim that:

Organisational perfection at one moment in time may well exclude future success, or to misquote, 'The price of survival is eternal vigilance if not paranoia.'

We accept that 'what needs to be done' to prosper in the future and 'what can be done realistically' are not the same thing, and certainly not the same thing for a manager working within an organisation. Suggesting change can be bad for one's organisational health and we will attempt to explain how the individual manager can choose the most appropriate strategy for personal and organisational survival and growth. We will also remind the reader that the moment in history when an organisation is most successful within its environment may be the best place to propose change but it is certainly not the easiest.

We see the effective organisation in analogy as a thriving tree. In the science of ecology we can study what makes one tree successful while other very similar trees wither and die. The ecologist does this by looking at the relationship between the tree, its own resources and the environment within which it finds itself, and we wish to apply the same process of thinking to organisations. By looking at an organisation's total environment we hope to see why some organisations appear to prosper while apparently similar organisations wither or are culled. By understanding the ecology of organisation we can begin to see how old growth can be removed and new growth stimulated, and we can also predict the time when the organisation ceases to be relevant within its world by looking at changes in the relevant ecology. The very special managers who are able to use their helicopter vision and can doctor, prune or indeed cull the organisational biosystems within which they live are rare and very often come from outside the organisation. The hostile take-over is the ultimate comment of the outsider on a failing organisation, the lumberjack of the logging company who sees a different use for the tree. This chapter is intended to allow you, our Aware Manager, to gain advanced warning of how an unbiased outsider with helicopter vision might see your company and allow you to take personally appropriate action.

So we may be vulnerable – where do I start looking?

The Ecology of Organisations

In the analogy, the Organisational Tree develops a symbiotic relationship with its surroundings. No two trees, and certainly not two trees of different species have exactly the same local environment of stones and mosses, lichens, squirrels and beetles. The exact growth and shape of each tree is modified by the weather and the type and amounts of the resources available to it. Each tree forms a micro-climate for the plants and animals under its influence. The tree uses resources – water, salts, air and sunshine, and uses them in a specific and ingenious way. The tree even makes use of the creatures living under its influence. The bees pollinate, squirrels carry away its seeds, and humble earthworms drag leaves underground to enrich the soil upon which the tree stands.

In the sense that a tree reacts to certain changes in its environment it could even be said to 'perceive' certain sorts of stimuli. The ecology of the tree is not static. New branches form and old branches wither. Amid life and death a stable ecology is re-established. However, the tree may become too demanding for its water supply or too heavy for its root anchors. The very earth upon which the tree depends may become eroded or the carbon dioxide and water of its life may become polluted to an acid poison. The tree may be dragged down by its parasites or simply become too old.

As it is with the tree, so it is with the organisation. The 'factors'

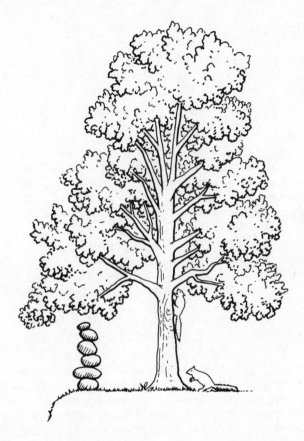

of the ecology of the tree are directly paralleled by those of the organisation. The organisation has the internal resources that provide basic stability and the external resources from suppliers and we have the various 'Fair Winds' that provide extra protections in bad times. However, unless the organisation and the tree adapt continuously to changes in their ecology they will die. Sometimes the changes are too profound and no adjustment or evolution is possible – the tree/organisation is out of its time.

Up to the late 1960s the Animal Feed companies of the UK used the by-products of the margarine industry for the bulk of their raw materials. Various forms of oil-bearing seeds were imported, from what is now termed 'the Third World' but what was then still thought of as 'the Colonies', and these seeds were processed to produce margarine with the nutritious husks compounded with small percentages of grains and other materials to make animal feeds. The margarine plants were naturally sited at the ports – Bristol, Liverpool and London – and the animal feed factories close by to reduce transport costs. It was a sound arrangement which allowed for the best balance of costs, transport and labour – the ecology was well defined.

The sound ecological balance was disrupted very soon after the Second World War. Marshall Aid and subsequent international schemes allowed the Third World countries to process their own oil seeds and export processed oils to the rest of the world. What now happened was that the vast *bulk* of the raw materials for animal feeds now consisted of grains being produced inland – perhaps at the very farms that were the subsequent market for the animal feed. Very little raw material came from the 'factory next door' as it produced its margarine.

A new set of mills appeared inland near to the farms with a new ecology of their own and the old port-based mills became uneconomic. The previous Fair Wind advantage of geography became a major on-cost to the port-based mills and they were driven to closure by the construction of a number of farming area located mills which were able to reduce transport costs to a minimum and achieve a sounder balance with their environment.

Successful companies live within an environment and often by their very size and structure establish a form of inertia that can well look ideal. The port-based animal feed compounders fought the more ecologically sound country-based mills by increasing their technical base – adding magic ingredients and by exploiting the conservative nature of their customers by sound brand names and good marketing, but the writing was on the wall and they foundered.

New companies may be protected like saplings in the fenced enclosures of tax havens but ultimately they will have to face the world. Like trees living in a National Park, some organisations survive by living in the protected environments of New Towns or Special Development Areas. The subsidies that allow National Parks or Special Development Areas can be withdrawn and the organisation, as it is with the tree, needs to fend for itself. Only the most perfectly adapting trees and the most perfectly adapting organisations survive.

Finally, and here we accept that the analogy of the tree breaks down, the organisation has to earn its place in the sun by giving service to a 'customer' of some kind. The 'customer' may be a public body or a small child spending its pocket money, but in the end the 'customer base' is the actual decision-maker in our economic systems. The customer base is, therefore, an organisation's greatest source of vulnerability. The aeroplane propeller-maker had its 'customer base' in the propeller-driven aeroplane business and when his customers turned to the jet engine it availed the manufacturer of propellers nothing, however the product was improved or cheapened to retain the business. When the 'customer base' goes, then the organisation is like a tree when the sea sweeps away its cliff – like so much driftwood on the beach. The organisation has fallen out of its time.

In looking at the 'customer base' we need to look at an important connecting link in the ecology of organisations; the social mores that join the 'basic need' and the 'customer base' and we will take for example a charitable trust designed to provide for orphans. As originally conceived the trust devoted its efforts to supplying special homes for underprivileged children. Its customer base existed in generous people who gave money to charities and agreed with the provision of institutional homes. If the Trust organisation does not accept that the revised social mores of the present day dictates a preference for maintaining families intact and is repelled by the concept of institutional homes, its 'customer base' and hence its funding will vanish. There will be more driftwood on the beach.

Our beginning point is that you, an Aware Manager, are working in a real organisation with its place in the real world and need to know the integral factors that make for present success. You need this information as a starting-point to planning your own and/or the organisation's survival and growth. Once you have defined the factors which contribute to present success, or got others in more authority to define them, you can take a rational view of the organisation's stability in the certainty that the world will change. In our tree analogy, you may only be one beetle on a vast oak, but knowing that the oak may wither and die should a particular wind change may allow you to decide on your personal future, unencumbered by the mind music of loyalty. Do you wish to stay and see your tree fall or do you wish to find a safer oak? At least you should have the choice.

In practice if we need to look at the 'ecology' of an organisation we are sensible to use some form of checklist and consult the opinion of senior management. What can emerge is a pattern – potential vulnerabilities which show in more than one area. It is

Checklist for the study of the ecology of an organisation

FACTOR	CHALLENGE	Scoring Scale of challenges 'S' 1–10 'C' 1–10

BASIC NEED
What is the basic need catered for by the organisation?

What threats can be envisaged to reduce this need?

OVERALL CLAIM TO SURVIVAL
Why this particular organisation for this need?

What threats will reduce this uniqueness?

INTERNAL RESOURCES
What internal resources does the organisation need to uphold its claim to survival? These can be collated as:
　FINANCIAL
　HUMAN
　SPECIAL SKILLS
　GEOGRAPHICAL

How could these internal resources be lost or reduced?

OUTSIDE RESOURCES
What outside resources are necessary for the operation? These can be collated as:
　FINANCIAL
　RAW MATERIAL
　SKILLS
　SPECIAL HELP
　SERVICES
　ENVIRONMENT

What could interfere with the availability of the outside resources?

PROTECTION
What special help does the organisation receive? Examples may include: Private, Local and Governmental

What factors could remove or reduce this special help?

CUSTOMER BASE

Who actually pays the bills?	How could this be threatened?

SOCIAL CONTEXT

What is the social context of the customer base and basic need?	How could the 'social context' be threatened? Upon what assumptions is it based?

the interactions that a wise organisation and its Aware Managers will monitor very carefully.

Our checklist will begin by taking the Basic Need the organisation fulfils and we will start by discussing the example of the animal feed companies. On an immediate level the **basic need** the companies filled was that of supplying feedstock to farmers. We may choose to develop this simple definition into the rather grand term – a **Mission Statement**, but at this point the short definition will suffice – THE REASON FOR THE ORGANISATION EXISTING AT ALL: *farmers needed feedstock supplement and the organisations were set up to supply them.* Next we have to question why *these* particular trees or organisations? What have these particular organisations to claim that sets them aside from other units in the same business? Next in our iconoclastic study we have to look inside the organisations themselves – what internal strengths did they have and how were these internal strengths augmented from the outside?

For the tree the internal resources might well be strong roots and a family of squirrels who spread its seeds. For the organisation they might be patents, strong financial reserves and friends in the city. Patents run out, financial reserves fall and friends become alienated. Our favoured tree and successful organisation is likely to have special protection – a sheltering wall or a preferential tax regime, but here, as we have said before, the analogy breaks down. The organisation has a particular source of finance – its customer base – and this, like many of the other factors in our organisational environment, exists in a social context. Each and every one of these factors is subject to Challenge and Threat, but we need to be realistic. We need to classify the Challenges against both chance of occurring and seriousness. Tidal waves are rare and are likely to be disastrous, while minor flooding is common but probably not serious.

In practice we would draw up a picture of the ecology of a real organisation using a checklist of some sort and prepare action plans using the decision-makers of the organisation. The basic checklist will need to be tailored to the exact profile of a particular organisation but the elements will remain the same.

Working with a real organisation, we suggest that the checklist is bespoke in a form that an aware senior manager would find reasonable. To apply the checklist in practice you need to be very clear on your own status in the organisation. If you are not in a senior enough position to determine or advise on the strategic course of your organisation, you may choose to attempt to influence a manager who is, but take care. You may choose to let them read this book and perhaps open the discussions informally, but do not push and be impatient. If you are in a sufficiently influential position I suggest that you designate a Middle Manager as a facilitator with special responsibility and make the importance you attach to the special assignment very clear – what is being done may well decide the future of the organisation. The designated facilitator needs to fix a date for a full day's meeting with all senior managers including yourself, and circulate a version of our bespoke checklist asking for written comments in advance.

The venue for the meeting would be in a private room and the discussions would begin with an explanation not only of their importance but also of their confidentiality. The facilitating manager will have already collated and structured the written comments from the group onto flip charts pinned to the walls of the room and these comments will be used as a basis to structure the meeting. Each Threat or Opportunity would be considered in turn and the 'Seriousness' and 'Chance of Occurring' columns of the charts would be completed. We are conducting a problem-solving meeting, concentrating on the *Why?* Questioning quadrant and are using a variation of Brainstorming.

What is likely to happen in our experience is that a global view of the Organisational Ecology emerges with about six areas worthy of study in depth. The Senior Managers then are able to take these areas and work on them as they see fit, moving from the Questioning quadrant through the Analysis and Practical quadrants towards Action. A small organisation could of course use a less formal approach – but the informality must not mask the seriousness of the enterprise.

To explain further let us set up a fictitious company and prepare the global view with its areas for further investigation.

The Company we will study is Motor Components Ltd (MCL). MCL is a relatively new company set up by its Managing Director when he realised that there was a gap in the 'Do-it-Yourself' (DIY) Car Accessory Business because of the vast complexity of European Safety Regulations. It is also fictitious. A local manufacturer, buying part-assembled components from the Third World and completing the assembly locally, would be more able to meet local laws. The factory is in a Development Area and the business is thriving. The Managing Director feels uneasy and wishes to make sure that his company will survive and prosper in the foreseeable future.

The Managing Director appoints a Middle Manager to run an Organisation Ecology Session and sets aside time for the board to co-operate. The checklist is circulated after a briefing session. It is made clear that the findings of the session are highly confidential and the total concept of the exercise has the Managing Director's direct backing.

The Table (page 170) shows how the results from the individual comments and the meeting could be assembled by the Middle Manager in a confidential memorandum to the board. The jargon is that of the company itself.

Summarising from the chart of the Ecology of Motor Components Ltd, we see that prudent management will be concerned in certain crucial areas:

(a) *The relative exchange rates between its home base and those of its suppliers.* Further study may show that some of the suppliers have completely artificial exchange rates which are subject to political whim. (2, 6)

(b) *Rival companies.* Either taking the market or the labour force. (5, 10)

(c) *The very special position of the present Senior Management.*

The special skills look as if they are indispensable and along with the loss of government protection in two years – the organisational tree may be planted in shallow ground. The dependence on 'credibility' to the Bankers for the main cash-flow emphasises the problem that is to come. (3, 7, 11, 12)

(d) *The Structure of DIY Retail Trade.* – Own brands, dependence on a few major customers and possible take-overs. (23, 24)

(e) *Unionisation preventing some of the mobility.* – Switching of

Organisational Ecology Session for Motor Components Ltd

BASIC PURPOSE OF ORGANISATION	CHALLENGE	S	C
		(1–10)	
1. To supply cheap 'safe' components to the DIY	The future of the car	10	1

OVERALL CLAIM TO SURVIVAL

2.	(a)	Supply of 'cheap bits' from Third World.	Exchange rates	10	6
3.	(b)	Contacts in Third World.	Sophistication of makers.	6	3
4.	(c)	Ability to assemble and sell to exact local standards.	World-wide standards.	9	3
5.	(d)	Local hero.	Real Local hero.	9	2

INTERNAL RESOURCES
MONEY

6. Overseas credits.	Exchange rates.	as 3	
7. Guaranteed supply of instant cash.	Lack of bank credibility.	10	3
8. Rapid contract repayment by trade.	Failure of large account.	7	5

HUMAN

9. Mobile full-time and part-time workers	Unionisation.	5	5
10.	Rival factory in area.	7	6
11. Entrepreneurial top management.	Age/illness.	8	9
12. Skilled initial local advice.	Lack of update.	8	7

SPECIAL SKILLS

13. Contacts.	Age, illness or time.	8	7
	International atmosphere.	6	5

GEOGRAPHIC ISSUES

14. New-town grants.	Policy change.	4	9

OUTSIDE RESOURCES
raw materials

15. Assemblies from Third World.	Quality control.	6	8
16.	Delays in supply.	6	5
17.	Wars, etc.	6	5
18. Plastic components.	Quality.	8	2

SKILLS
19. Legal/local advice and contacts. See 13.

SERVICE
20. Heat, water, security, transport. Social disorder. 6 5

ENVIRONMENT
21. Factory conditions. New housing. 5 6

OUTSIDE PROTECTION
22. Subsidised rates/rent in New Town. see 14.

CUSTOMER BASE
23. DIY Supermarkets Own brands. 8 5
24. Concentrations in retailers. 8 8
25. Entry by major. 8 9

SOCIAL CONTEXT
26. Private motoring – car as status symbol. Electric car. 5 5
27. Hire/rental 2 9
28. Third World cheap labour. Changes. 10 6

 lines and flexibility of working hours, in the workforces. (9)

(f) *The vulnerability of supplies* from particular Third World countries suggesting that alternative supply sources should be considered. (2, 15, 16, 17, 20, 28)

In the meeting this form of summary should be made by the Middle Manager running the discussion, and the board left to detail action – What needs to be done, what needs to be watched, what contingency action needs to be taken. Because action can seem imperative to a dispassionate observer does not mean that the persons directly concerned will take such action. Consider point (c) where the Senior Executive may be vitally concerned on a personal level with the comments – *it may be the Senior Executive the meeting is talking about.* The board now has enough Adult information for them to monitor the changes in the organisation environment and take reasonable action. The action may not, in the most unfavourable set of circumstances, save the company, but the action may well prevent all but a freak wave sweeping away the corporate cliff.

Woe betide any Middle Manager who attempts to put across any changes that conflict directly with the Senior Executives on a personal level without their prior and tacit understanding. Very few Senior Managers are *that* aware.

However, in the whole history of forecasting it is said that nobody has ever over-estimated the time a change needs to take effect or on the other hand over-estimated the consequences *when* the change has occurred. We advise caution in any predictions, particularly if you are associated with them, and worse still if you could be seen to gain personally by any of your 'advice'.

During the meeting and the subsequent analysis, the Aware Middle Manager may realise that there are certain sensitive areas – basic assumptions that are dangerous to challenge within the organisation. These we term **core concepts** and we need to discuss how an Aware Manager determines these issues which may well become sticking-points. By knowing the core concept of the organisation the Aware Manager may be able to facilitate effective evolution or be able to recognise that the corporate tree is too old or too set in its ways to change. It is then for the individual manager to consider alternative action.

Suppose in our example of MCL the senior management initiated the investigation but you still feel you need to know some more of the politics to phrase the report diplomatically and effectively. The organisation, or at least the body of individuals representing it, still needs to be told and still needs to listen.

Understanding the Core Concepts of an Organisation

The reader may already know my favourite quotation on change:

> There is nothing more difficult to take in hand, more perilous to conduct, or more uncertain in its success, than to take the lead in the introduction of a new order of things, because the innovator has for enemies all those who have done well under the old conditions, and lukewarm defenders in those who may do well under the new.

> Machiavelli (1446–1507), *The Prince*

Any large or medium-sized organisation tree is complex and any change will be interactive and the simplistic Spinning Plate approach of Chapter 7 can only structure our thought process.

⟶

EXERCISE

Imagine our motor components company deciding to change its packaging for a part of its product range. Instead of simple boxes with the part numbers visible on the narrow short face, supermarket shelves demand a bubble-pack able to hang from a peg in a stand controlled, owned and serviced by MCL itself. List the changes the pack modifications will make – think of the chain from manufacturing, packing in the factory, warehousing, distribution, stocktaking, delivery, stock-control and selling.

⟶

In our example very little can still be assumed but unless the change is viewed logically and in a structured way, many issues will be missed. When you made your list, had you considered the quality control issue of the customer being able to *see* the product clearly before purchase? A brainstorming session might yield dozens of other unexpected consequences of varying importance but remember the change we initiated was apparently very small – a simple change in product packaging. Imagine the following scenario where the *Purpose* plate of an organisation is altered:

A major children's charity was established at the end of the nineteenth century and controlled through the Methodist assembly. Its original purpose was to give Christian shelter to the homeless waifs of the industrial cities, and in that purpose it thrived for nearly a hundred years. Many things changed in that time, and these changes certainly included the social welfare programmes of the 1950s in the UK, but the charity lived and evolved with the changes. It ran homes within and alongside the state-sponsored systems.

In the middle 1980s it was decided that the evolution was not enough and that the problems of the inner cities could not be tackled on a purely Christian basis. A multi-cultural approach was demanded.

The reader may like to speculate on the changes such a move in purpose involves. Using the Spinning Plate approach we can see that virtually no aspect of the organisation remains unaltered and certainly the change was traumatic for many of the staff. Part-time and notionally paid workers suddenly found themselves facing stresses that even our toughest readers would regard as 'experiences'. The charity has survived, but as in an old TV soap opera – 'Even the name has been changed to protect the innocent.'

Change invoked by movements in the social context of the organisation may well shake the very central structure: in our analogy of the tree – the very trunk and roots. If we *have* to put in change to survive – and we do – it is wise to understand not only the ecology of the organisation tree but also its Core Concepts – WHAT IS THE FUNDAMENTAL THINKING BEHIND THE ORGANISATION?

In practice we have found two ways of looking at the Core Concepts of Organisations, the first is fun and highly creative. The second is coldly clinical. The choice of technique will depend on you and the audience you may have to convince of your discovery. Let's try the 'Fun' method first.

We call this the PERSONIFICATION METHOD and in it we think of the organisation as a person. It might be difficult to think of how to approach an organisation and give it bad news, how much easier would it be if we could think of a person that *feels* the same way as the organisation and tell them.

EXERCISE

We already know quite a bit about Motor Components Ltd.

Look back on the data you already have on the organisation and attempt to describe it in ten adjectives. Forget it is a company employing people, and existing with factory gates, try to see it as a *person*.

Look back on the list and attempt to give a name to that person.

(Characters in fiction or Nursery Rhyme are particularly useful.)

In using this exercise we have found many adjectives used and the ones we have chosen come into two sets – only an insider would be able to make the choice as to which set was more apposite. An outsider without that knowledge could well make a considerable error in approaching the organisation if he or she made the wrong choice.

Two sets of adjectives for MCL as a person:

Brash	Neat
Pushy	One Man Band
Adolescent	Small
Manipulative	Resilient
Smart Alec	Patriotic
Exploiting	Model

Obviously, the adjectives on the left relate to a different company to those on the right. Those on the left might be represented by the character of early James Cagney movies and the ones on the right by David of David and Goliath fame. Only people intimate with MCL will be able to make the decision and finger the character of the organisation.

Equally obviously, changes proposed and accepted by the fictional James Cagney organisation will be different from those accepted by one symbolised by the Davids of this world. The person proposing changes is well advised to know with whom he or she is dealing.

> Tracy Kidder in his book *Soul of a New Machine* describes the world of Data General. He quotes two company advertisements – one used and one confined to folklore.
>
> 'I'm Ed Castro, President of Data General Corporation. Seven months ago we started the richest small computer company in history. This month we're announcing our first product: the best small computer in the world . . . Because if you're going to make a small inexpensive computer you have to sell a lot of them to make a lot of money. And we intend to make a lot of money.'
>
> And an unused advertisement still on the President's wall stated when IBM announced their entry to the world of mini-computers at that time dominated by DEC and Data General:
>
> 'They say IBM's entry into mini-computers will legitimise the market. The bastards say, WELCOME.'

I think we can say that Data General saw itself as a James Cagney type of organisation, and any employee who wished to stay working with Ed Castro needed to learn that pretty fast – changes involving diplomacy might be very difficult to put over; don't expect sympathy.

The Davids in the world would be small companies who have

evolved a niche in a market dominated by vast multinationals. Perhaps Croda International would see itself in that light against the ICI's, Unilever's and General Goods. Here loyalty as opposed to machismo is necessary to survive.

EXERCISE

Go through the previous exercise for your own organisation.

Are the changes you feel needed by your organisation the sort of things you could propose to the individual you feel encapsulates the character of *your* organisation?

Does the character you see in your organisation give you any insight into problems you may have had in proposing change into your organisation?

During our work with groups of managers using this technique we have come across many strange characters masquerading as organisations:

James Bond. The Senior Manager saw himself as an 'M' character trying to control a talented but irresponsible genius. As his organisation pillaged its way with blameless charm its Manager found himself picking up the pieces.

The Exploring Caterpillar. We have an image of a slow and ponderous organisation chewing its way in a comparatively aimless manner. In pursuing the analogy the manager even considered the possibility of a metamorphosis into a lovely butterfly.

God. This serious analogy was derived by a Manager of rich endowment in the States. The allocation of funds was almost god-like and could literally mean life or death to the supplicant. As the analogy developed, we found that the pet names for people and places fitted the character of God. The main entrance hall, for example, was called the mausoleum and the chief executive – the high priest.

Second-Hand Rose. Here the Manager worked for a subsidiary of a large company and felt that everything she had to work with – materials as well as people – were cast-offs. We will meet her again.

The serious aspect of the creative study of organisations as people is that it gives us a truly global view of organisational personality. We can ask how the exploring caterpillar or Bond or Second-Hand Rose or James Cagney would accept a particular change or modification. Things that would not even be noticed by the James Cagney personification – like replacing tea ladies with vending machines – might be earth-shattering for the 'exploring caterpillar'.

Having explained the fun method of attempting to understand an organisation, we should restore confidence by explaining the clinical method. The method is a version developed by Edward de Bono in his book *Lateral Thinking for Management*. His words are not exactly those of our checklist but run parallel. Thus we used the terms **Basic Need** and **Overall Claim of Uniqueness**. Although de Bono and later Peters used the concept of **Purpose** and **Mission Statement**, the concepts have much in common.

Firstly the **Purpose** or **Mission Statement** of the organisation is given in a succinct statement:

e.g. for our fictitious organisation Motor Components Ltd, the purpose might read:

> The purpose of the Company is to supply cheap 'Safe' components to the DIY Motor Parts Business by purchasing part-completed bits from Third World countries and assembly to meet precise and local safety legislation.

The second stage of our logical analysis is to look at the individual words and phrases in the 'job description' and question the implication behind them. The point of the word and phase questioning exercise is to become clear on what we have decided to exclude, as well as include, in our concept of the organisation. For example let us look at the word 'cheap' and what lies behind its use in the 'job description'. In our mind's eye we see a positioning of our products in the low-cost sales area of the market-place. By this vision we may be as F. W. Woolworth was and be, perhaps, similarly trapped in the high competition end of the 'small profits quick return' business. The assumptions of the word 'cheap' are very far-reaching and as such are obviously very vulnerable to a multitude of factors in the outside world.

In practice we would suggest that you ask to run an audiotape meeting with the managers of your organisation using the 'job description' as an agenda of the discussion. Set a definite limit in time for the discussion and promise a written and frank analysis in the next week. The analysis for MCL could well look something like this:

Analysis of MCL Core Concepts – de Bono system

Word under scrutiny	What is implied	What is excluded	What threats or opportunities lie in the exclusions
Cheap	We compete on price alone	Competition on quality of brand	Margins. Own brands. R&D to maintain position.
	We are seen to be the bottom in status	Any form of pride	Can we achieve product differentiation? Parsimony can well spread to the workplace.
			Should we sub-contract further?
Components to the DIY trade	We imply components to finished cars	We exclude components to manufacturers of the cars themselves	The social volatility of the DIY business.
Motor Parts	Motor Cars	Motor Bikes	Possibly a new market since nearly all Motor Cycles are imported and spares are correspondingly very expensive.

The de Bono analysis may come up with the same issues as the Ecology study but it will also come up with opportunities.

Understanding the 'ecology', the 'personality' and the 'core concepts' of an organisation allows us to take a dispassionate view of the organisation which provides the Aware Manager with his or her daily bread. We can understand what makes our organisation tick and what needs to be done to keep it ticking into the future. We can also take a very aware view on how best to advise for change and the likelihood of advice being taken.

Lever Industrial grew in the shadow of the mighty Lever Brothers and was readily personified by some of its senior management as 'Second-Hand Rose'. Originally developed as a company by the founders to deal with surplus washing products from its bigger brother, it began to feel its strength and in the mid-1970s the senior management conducted a complete analysis on the lines suggested in this chapter. The 'new image' was presented in an imaginative form at a company presentation in the Grand at Eastbourne – by no means a 'Second-Hand Rose' environment. The presentation was structured so that it was supposed to be ten years in the future and the Eastbourne conference was discussed as if it had a place in company history as a turning-point of the company image. The changes that the company had put through in the intervening ten years were detailed as fact. The response of the conference to the perhaps rather unconventional method of suggesting a change of company core concepts and image was mixed, and the response of the sales force in particular was less than understanding. Some three months later the author met the senior executive by chance in a restaurant and was told that 'he had been thinking about that presentation'. One year later the author was invited to a display of the company products. It was superb, bright and witty with no sign of 'Second-Hand Rose', except for one dull sack of industrial dishwasher product in the corner.

'Sorry about that, it's the only one we haven't got round to.'

Second-Hand Rose at least had one product that she would have recognised.

EXERCISE

The Navy is often called 'the Mob', IBM is 'Big Blue' and Shell is known as 'Joe Shell'. How would the familiar names of these companies reflect on the styles of management within them? How is your own company known?

Using either the 'creative' or the 'analysis' method of looking at your own organisation, come to a view on its Core Concepts.

Think of these Core Concepts in terms of your own valued
skills and in terms of the times you have found your advice,
in perhaps a wider context than your actual job, has either
been welcomed or lost to the desert air.

———————————➤

In our last chapter we will attempt to summarise a long journey
that hopefully will allow you to be more personally effective by
understanding what you value and upon what you derive no
satisfaction – what is for you neither possible nor useful. We may
also have allowed you space to pack a parachute.

CHAPTER TEN

Write Three Envelopes

The final chapter of our book will contain two stories, one to open the discussion and one to close the book.

Once upon a time a manager was appointed to take over a department from a manager leaving in disgrace. In the lobby as the incoming manager moved towards the lift he was greeted by the cheery voice of his predecessor:

'If you ever get into trouble, look into the second drawer of the desk. You will find three envelopes, and you open the first.'

The incoming manager was surprised but did note that there were three envelopes neatly labelled in the order they had to be opened. He thought nothing more about it until, after a series of bad situations, he found himself called to a board meeting to defend his record. He went back to the drawer and opened the first envelope.

'This is the message of the first envelope. You are obviously in trouble but do not worry – it was all your predecessor's fault – blame me.'

All was well at the board meeting and everyone joined in rubbishing the previous manager, but in the six months after the meeting things went from bad to worse. The manager thought again of the envelopes and opened the second:

'Do not worry. The message of the second envelope is to blame the prevailing state of the world economy. "Nobody could have done better, but you know how it is . . ." sort of thing.'

At the latest board meeting the manager was able to gather sympathy and soon everyone present was blaming everyone else and even the 'Greenhouse Effect'.

Life and times got worse and after a further six months our manager was summoned again, and again he went to the drawer, this time for the last envelope. The message now, in his time of need was:

'Write three envelopes.'

The Aware Manager must always be prepared to write three envelopes but I hope we have shown a better way of facing the future. In our time together we have explained about the honeymoon period where we adapt ourselves to the job. During that period it is unlikely that somebody does not wish to give us a chance and covertly or overtly we will be allowed to blame those who went before. In the first chapter we went beyond the stage of development and began to look at the way we are likely to manoeuvre the priorities of the job towards employing the skills that we personally value. We took the skills of Betty, crisis manager and Campbell, a steady soul, and showed how they might well develop the same job, in spite of the job's accepted and understood definition, in completely different ways towards giving each of them personal satisfaction. We asked you, the reader, to list your own valued skills and see how you by a gentle selection of these in preference to less valued skills might move your own job towards personal satisfaction but not perhaps towards acceptance by the 'powers that be'. We then moved on to discussing how your behaviour may well change fundamentally under stress conditions and how this movement could well produce management problems for you and your staff if not understood. Betty of our first chapter moved in stress from an exciting if perhaps erratic manager to a strict and defensive one, while Campbell moved from a firm and clear management style to a behaviour that could be described as a 'manipulative social worker'. We have met many other managers who change style under stress and certainly the most common strategy is a movement towards an isolationist position. In looking at your own likely movement from the comfortable and perhaps most developed position towards the more untested stressed position we asked you to consider what could be done to make life easier and more effective for you, and your staff.

In the next two chapters we considered how the stresses that make us act inappropriately can be codified and reduced. The basic techniques for what is often called 'Assertiveness Training' amounted, in our discussion, to buying time while we review the mush of inappropriate messages in our heads. These inappropriate messages, which we termed Mind Music, could be so insistent that we relied on 'outside forces' to solve our own personal problems or so confusing and deafening as to prevent effective action altogether. The point at which we closed our discussion on assertiveness techniques was that in a world of aggressors the assertive is often avoided – being assertive and acting appropriately is quite often perceived through the eyes of others as a form of insubordination and may well lead to immediate troubles.

The next chapter dealt with the issues of the Aware Manager at meetings. We looked at the meta agenda of the meeting – the demonstration of power and control, the dissemination of information, the sharing of decision responsibility and problem-solving. We saw that the meeting was more effective if the meta agenda was made public and that perhaps the formal chaired meeting was not the best tool the Aware Manager could use, once the purpose of the meeting was understood. The possibility of alternatives to the chaired meeting was seen as particularly important in meeting the objectives of Problem-Solving. With Problem-Solving we saw phases which we named Why? – What? – How? and If? stages, each of which required a particular thinking style from the participants. The synthetic encouragement of the four stages could be by the use of particular techniques, but we saw individuals who fell naturally into these four styles of thinking. Chapter 7 discussed the consequences of the four styles of thinking to the perception of the management and to the roles of manager in interviewing and recruitment.

Chapter 8 moved away from the issues of the individual manager and his or her direct relations with staff. We considered how the selective employment of valued skills impinged on the way you as a manager operate. We saw the total management job as one of keeping a number of plates spinning simultaneously. The manager who fails to keep a weather eye on all the plates, all the time, will soon find him or herself 'writing the three envelopes'.

Chapter 9 developed a system by which you, as an Aware Manager, could look beyond the alligators of the day-to-day problems and remember that your actual purpose was originally to drain the swamp. The chapter also put forward the heresy that sometimes the job is impossible given the resources at your disposal.

We have come a long way in our nine chapters and we expect no conversion on the road to Damascus. By doing the job that little bit better, by not failing repeatedly for the same reason, by realising that *you* are responsible for your own fate and that 'outside forces' are excuses and not reasons, you can become an Aware Manager. The fractional improvement, and I think that even a 10 per cent increase in effectiveness would be remarkable, will help to increase your own personal motivation out of all proportion.

The only point I would like to leave you with is that the Aware Manager is not only aware of him or herself. The Aware Manager is fortunate in a moment of history, and for a moment only. Those around may be less fortunate.

> There is a legend about an African tribe many years ago. It was a custom in this tribe that the young warriors would throw their fathers over the edge of a high cliff when they ceased to be useful to the group.
>
> One day, at the high spot of the ceremony a young chief had taken his unprotesting father in a fireman's lift to the appointed place when he stopped.
>
> 'Why are you laughing father? This is a serious business.'
>
> 'Son, I was remembering the day I threw my father over.'

Good Luck!